CELLE FANTASTIK

Also by Adam Engel

Topiary: A Novel (2009)

I Hope My Corpse Gives You the Plague: My Life in the Bush Era of Ghosts (2010):

CELLA FANTASTIK

by

ADAM ENGEL

http://www.oliveropenpress.com

The Oliver Arts & Open Press

All rights reserved. No part of this book may be used or reproduced in any manner without written permission from the Publisher, except in the case of brief quotations that may appear in articles and reviews.

Engel, Adam, 1965-1985
Cella Fantastik

ISBN: 978-0-9829878-3-4
Library of Congress Control Number: 2010942591

The Oliver Arts & Open Press
2578 Broadway, Suite #102
New York, NY 10025
http://www.oliveropenpress.com

Cover & Interior Design by Bonita Rutigliano

DEDICATION

For 105 East Palisade Avenue and the spirits therein.

Onward—

to Jericho

—turn right
past the
"Palm at the End of the Mind,"
Exit 40—

(mind) State of
internal internecine
struggle without end
but still
it is possible to
liberate the robins
from larger, less forgiving trees

And in his geere for al the world he ferde,
Nat oonly lik the loveris maladye
Of Hereos, but rather lyk manye,
Engendred of humour malencolik,
Biforen, in his celle fantastik.*
And shortly, turned was al up so doun
Bothe habit and eek disposicioun
Of hym, this woful lovere daun Arcite.
The Knight's Tale, lines 1372-1379

* (pron: **chay** *lah fahn tahs* **teek**)
This has reference to the old division of the brain into three cells, the front one commonly assigned to fantasy, the middle one to reason, and the back one to memory. Mania was described as an affection of the first. . . . But Chaucer. . . apparently referred to the entire front cell as the *celle fantastik*.
—*The Works of Geoffrey Chaucer*, ed. F. N. Robinson

CONTENTS

Build Me a Tent 13
Creed of Core 15
Adieu 21
Abduction 22
After the After 23
American Duchess Waits For Spring 24
News and Improved: Rumors of Extinction Greatly Exaggerated 25
Between Nothing and Forever 26
Big Bang 27
Sang Body Electric 28
Carbon .30
Clock Speed 31
Cocaine Sonata 32
Cult Wired Hard 33
Ode to Cupid, Psyche, Herb 34
Déja Vu Again 36
Depart From Consume 37
Desert Law and Write-Ins 39
Dreams Like Memories 40
Earth Day 43
Ectomorph 44
End Day Kiss 46
Goodbye Alaska 48
Home Entertainment 49
Immortal Fictions 51
Less Than 53
Mannish Eyes 54
Commercial Brake 55
Great American MEme 56
The Mouse of Anarchy 57
A Nostrum for Your Senescence, or Death by Cartoon 58
Perpetual Yearning to Be You 60
Sherman Flame and Slaughter 61

Still Life Motor Inn With Prom Queen	.62
Still Life with Tentacle	.64
Sum	.67
"Ah hah! Pronoun trouble."—Daffy Duck	.67
Road Puppet Night Core	.68
Tête de Cinéma	.69
Regardless	.70
Repetition	.71
ROI	.72
The Ledge	.74
To the Bone	.77
Underground	.78
The Long, Unhappy Globalization of Variable x	.79
Vroom, vroom Beautiful!	.81
Westerners Dream Araby	.84
Write After Eternal	.85
Ball-peen Oratory	.86
Killing Time	.87
Here	.89
The Science of Forbidding Fruit	.90
Our Own	.91
Ready, Able, Fire	.93
Unfamiliar as a Stranger's Dream	.94
Phantom the Hotel	.95
Beneath Us	.96
Program	.97
Dark Above Her	.99
A Very Brady Homeland (the lost episodes, circa 1968-73)	101
Abraham & Franz	107
Let Me Bequeath	108
Corpus: Language of the Future	109
CODA	110

CELLA FANTASTIK

Build Me a Tent

Build me a tent. I'll throw a party for my friends, dead and living.

Silverware and China. Linen, glassware, corn poppers and cotton candy on the great lawn under stars (I used to think they were just props and scenery, the stars, but now I believe, I mean really *believe*, they're real).

Build me a tent; I'll throw a shindig under god.

Creed of Core

I. *Revery*

Perhaps answers in silence, the gray area outside of argument, beyond belief systems instilled in us (what we believe). Something more rootical than "reform." Action? When has anyone ever acted, not merely of conviction, but with consequence? I recall only cacophony. Our imagined "right" to call noise music when we were young things with immortal bodies, stoned on our bicycles past midnight. Invisible cricket chorus pleasant score. Done now, well and be done with it for good.

Were we ever outside the arena? All that star gazing, consumed by anxiety, futurity, desire. Reached for "good life." Our delicate fix. Learned our lines and towed them, dreaming guns and type-writers, mechanical genius of The Nation. Stuff and Nonsense. Stuff, stuff and more stuff. Ter-rif-fic.

Dear Diary: today I mourn the vanished. Vanquished. Synonymous, no?

Lies, lies, promises: "once I'm settled again I'll send for you, dear, and the children," such such such and so forth.

Anyway who can afford all this beginning-ness, everything so new, yet not improved? Upgraded. Maybe a few corrections. Slight.

Send it back, all of it. We haven't got all day, or all that many days. Call the supervisor. Demand the earth stop spinning. Talk, talk and more talk. Demand balcony tickets to the stars. Demand warm beds on which to plot beginnings. Real this time. Death is the song played over and over, Death and his brother, Work. I refuse to labor for cavilers and creeps. For what will I be rising and for whom? More importantly, *why?*

I get eye-strain. I have cramps. I'm claustrophobic and this cubicle is killing me. All I ever do is reach for phones. Enough! I was green yesterday, today I'm blue. Tomorrow brown as mud. I'm thin. Not too thin. But thin. Why shouldn't I expect the world?

In reverie I vanquish, always.

II. *Pleasures*

We had our pleasures too, of course. If music be the food of love, we feasted, feasted, gorged. Electric Guitar. Phallic fetish of our century. Crude talk of the folk. Jargon, slang, "hip-talk," double negatives and all, amplified, distorted, turned in upon itself. Crossroad blues of dark origins bleached, and branded "Rock n' Roll." Louder than airplanes, louder than opinions, louder than traffic. Cacophonous prayers of Limeys, Negroes, long-haired freaks summoned young gods who lived among us briefly, brashly. Pop salvation, "instant karma" for the young.

Guitar said, "Fuck you, big man."

Guitar said, "Shake for me."

Guitar said, "Listen."

Guitar said, "Walk away."

Guitar said, "Who are you."

Guitar said, "Lick me."

Guitar said, "Do it."

And whatever it was, we did, the young, for a while at least, when we heard Guitar (ubiquitous: how could we not?), knew its patois like a second tongue upon our cocks and cunts and in our throats.

It was our lyre.

But Power would have none of it.

They taught us to read books that our disease might wither. Pain management. Nobody wants to be depressed. So, if you look at all sides you'll have that many angles. Persistence decides these things. Agitprop. Hypnosis. Look at that man long enough, he'll fade away.

But imagine something terrible. Then what'll you do? And then what are you talking about? And then what you were dreaming? That girl in the hall turned on by photographs, celebrity fanzine stuff, not nightmares, nor visions of stick-men and great white spermy aliens like eye-less sharks.

"Doctor, careful, forceps…"

What histories will she deliver, what dead man pulled from her gray – takes awhile to download; some of the women are quite – when he comes home the children; when she admonishes the lamp. Supper time and consummate. We sop the blood with cake…

It ends with alarm. The television listens. It's about seven.

Simple: you just don't go. Have your mother write a note. Or your wife.

"Not here. Not this time." Better yet: "Can't I ever just relax?"

And upon the scene arrived the fire brigade. "Do you have any idea how he fell in to that well?"

Life without consequence.

Like in Kindergarten. Ms. Mulhollander dissected a Praying Mantis… belly full of indigestible, iridescent wings…

"Children, say 'thorax.' Say, 'abdomen.'"

It was dead already or she wouldn't have cut it.

"Killing a Praying Mantis is illegal. They help mankind."

Did we really want our teacher to do time?

After school we scorched ants under a glass.

"We have unleashed the power of the Sun upon Japan."

Nauseating stench. The lucky ones worked, dismantling a beetle.

"Arbeit Macht Frei!"

"An ant can carry 500 times its own weight."

Something like that. Good of the colony.

"Their lives suck. There, get that one!"

Fry 'em.

Surely we'll be punished. Official reprimand signed by Ms. Mulhollander herself, copied, filed among our permanent records.

I remember love notes folded in pieces, place marks for anthologies of Great and Famous Men, so many I lost count. Poems, essays, stories, notes. Words relating courage to believe in (even after what was written) worlds outside this room. If you would simply close the door on fetal life; bowls of plums; harsh angles, misunderstood by outside, outside gulped by in; believability in tatters, awaiting yet another Fall.

Why, only yesterday we mumbled whatever about how young they were when we last met, and all that pap about time flying, raging against incorrigible truth ("his daughter done him wrong" etc.).

Crying won't solve anything. You have to face…

"There, there," pat on the back. "Now, now."

But once it's reached the point of Free Delivery; of Future enfolded within Past; of marking time with cigarettes; of wanton soup; Fajitas; chrysaloid petals tucked dry, without wings…you must —

— reality delimited small real estate, chunks of earth and ash, cluttered apparatus. And again the matter of self.

"I can't face my reflection without thinking, 'No, no, it can't be…'"

Has Time been cruel, or did we expect too much?

Sipping cups of Yesterday to dregs of Winter.

"Fix me rum-and-chocolate, I'll be good as new…"

Our just desserts: to be aware of it all, to watch it happen, to be helpless, human.

"I'm not particularly afraid of myself, though I have been labeled dangerous…"

We're unhappy. We'll die. We'll be forgotten.

"The liquid me, the meat."

Turning heads of old men in the park, fucking lovers senseless as we wandered in and out of Time.

"I'm human. I have every right to be forgiven…"

Don't go there now. Why speak of it?

"It's easy, like riding a bicycle…"

No hands, imbalanced, credulous, unfocused. Children of faith.

"Simple, see? You just let go…"

III. *Promises*

Regardless of what "society was founded on" and blah blah blah, deep human defies despised abilities: a third way, a fourth, a fifth. But we can have our dialogue with Time, our argument with Time, our diatribe against Time, at any time. We can say, you know, "Just stop. Cease. Desist. Scram," and that's completely.

We will know the pleasant smell of skin; new beginnings will entice us to rise, still, yet, again, despite perceived redundancies of morning (we shall unlearn them into novelties, ecstasies), pleasure the first thing on our minds.

I ask you to take another look. The Painters dare not startle us with stark imago, for outdoors we are safe. It is (has always been, really) in our power to elude sophisticated instruments, come face to face with Angels (note: NOT flat-foot tattle-tales of yore, spooks, gumshoes of The (alleged) Almighty, "friendly" surveillance 24/7, up to no good and probably forever, but lusty, meaty spirits like ourselves).

Listen to me: don't fear the next line. Masturbate, soliloquize, expose yourself, defy Leviathans of logic, again and again and again, even unto The Reckoning.

The Judgment, so much hype and ballyhoo, can be, must be, our blessing. Only latency, for now; not specifically "what God decreed," unless red smolders pink and even roar-fire youth reduced by bureaucrats and cynics to a hiccup, cough in Time, mere phase or fad.

Perverse obsession to be led. No. No.

Never. Never. Never. Never. Never.

"I don't know what you're talking about," she said. "The psychic told me I've no aura. She looked at my palm and said that. She doesn't know how I lost my aura, it's just gone. At ten bucks a year she would research my life to find out where my aura went to, which isn't so bad on the surface, but she brought up the possibility of 'pre-birth' experiences, past lives. It could cost me, this psychic doctorate of hers. 'Apply for a grant,' I told her. Madame Kava Kava or Java Beans or something like that. I didn't really get her name. I tossed her card.

Why? You really want to see her?"

We shared a cigarette before the dance. And no one else in her peculiar perfume, t-shirt, boxer shorts and pointy boots, her Panama hat and hyacinth tattoo. When beauty doesn't merely knock, but batters down the door. We recognize such moments in association with music, whatever's playing in the background, and olfactory stimulants. Hopelessly nostalgic for moments never known. Sooner or later she'll wise up to all that. Didn't you?

Possibly, in some later innocence, our clean future, we'll abandon rubbers. Hortatory of libido, Cupid's counsel: skin-on-skin, our skin, not latex or cellophane or whatever they'll sell you in those corny packages: "Night Star," "Rough Rider" "Pure Sensation" "Dive on in." Cold barrier. Like fucking a mackerel.

Desire to say something meaningful a dead weight on your tongue. Even before Ovid (in translation), or Keats (as if she'd stepped out of an ode), I knew plain longing, unfinished union, promise of beauty deferred…

So don't say "can't get any better than this," because it will.

Adieu

Witnessed before tumors spread like chicken-pox. Diaries kept. Accept, adjust, return.

Witness to airplane days of fly me I'm Linda, fly me, I'm Gail. Beware physicians and their hypnogogic bed-size banner.

"Needless overhead," said the CFO, a CPA, to the CEO, who related their conclusion to the bored. Boredom: Karmic tax imposed upon obscene wealth. Blasé omnipotence of digital transactions: nine figures, ten figures, eleven (yawn), twelve. No cold cash or coin. No gold, no sop, no taters.

The next great train robbery walked off with someone's – dare I say whose? --wireless contraption and personal digital assistant (who'll offer no resistance, unlike buxom Gal Fridays of corporate yore).

What's with these Yanks of today, all hard-bone-cold-snot-and-marrow?

Yet all is not completely lost. You – assuming you are – must do what "Mother" Nature sez and "clean your damned room!"

Adieu.

Abduction

It was not like TV at all. I mean, it seemed unreal.

Sure, there were the typical bright lights and loss of time-sense, but who hasn't experienced that particular mind-zap on a week-night? Awake suddenly three hours before the nasty clock-radio-alarm, dreading the inevitable approach of "reveille" — damn digital alarm clock-radio/time-bomb the most dreadful techno-majig this side of the stun-gun? No, it was the talk, the screechy-scratchy space gossip of the so called "aliens" that indicated "this ain't Kansas, Toto," really freaked me out. High-pitched, "crunchy," sounds; like insects talking, debating about god knows what.

Didn't help my overall emotional condition that I was paralyzed, mute, and positioned in such a way as to be unable to avert my gaze from the neat rows of sharp instruments on what appeared to be a very hard, very cold table.

And of course (of course: what would an "abduction" be without an intimate invasion/violation with anti-septic, phallic instruments?) telescoped long, steely gadgets up my wazoo.

They "beamed me back" or however they transported me, exactly one minute before the first gush of clock-radio muzak, which lasted an eternity, for I was too messed up to slam the "snooze button," at six a.m. Cruel bastards. Yes, there is "intelligent life," beyond the solar system and yes it is every bit as diabolical as anything that walks terrestrial legs.

And the ultimate question: was it a dream? No. No way. They left, as proof, tiny scoop marks on my thigh. I'm sure, for their purposes, these were more than just souvenirs. Was I being cataloged, a data-unit on some intergalactic spread-sheet?

Regardless: onward. To the shower, the espresso pot, the car my pod my womb. Two hours in traffic and another fifteen minutes to find parking. May I not collapse on the packed pavement of my destination or drop dead in the cubicle, unremarked till pay day or stink of personal decay or impromptu staff meeting.

May I survive this day's abduction, return home again, home again to night's dull channels, or perhaps a movie, catatonic lifetimes past unspeakable probes and alien chit-chat in unidentified fleeting objects of deliverance.

After the After

So in this Nation of celebrities; schnooks; has-beens; never-beens; writers; programmers; hackers; convicts; executives; serfs, Information Architects and all manner of Data manipulators and killer-cop-thieves, a Nation too big for one to know, much less understand, he was walking with a friend, young and ebullient on the asphalt – no; that was years ago, actually, many years ...experience, on the ebullient... asphalt...

All men are common who have not found their voice. He has not found his voice in the wake of this riotous din. He keeps to himself, as far as possible from the hoi-polloi and their gadgets, gizmos, baubles. A thinking man seeks peace.

But does it matter after (there's always an "after," when no one recalls the doings of his forebears), and after that after, after the final after, when we're sucked into blackness-blankness, where actions are not marked, nor deeds recorded?

Does it matter after curves in space, the next bird, if he was a master of dialog and faith, a poet, who dug deep, slept fitfully, and eventually –

American Duchess Waits For Spring

The coca leaf makes lovely tea. Laudanum in rosewater. But when you concentrate and manufacture, process, condense into concoctions, you lose essential properties to gain – what? what is it, what? What is it you want of Life it obviously cannot (will not?) give?

Our captains of industry, Your shareholders and CEOs; Our entrepreneurs, Your technocrats and managers; Our hard machinery, Your delicate gadgets "crunching" numbers unto bland abstraction.

Your "hectic modern lifestyle..."

Heaven help you and your cartoon Nietzsche, cut-and-paste Marx; your quarter billion dead and maimed. Your managers fiddle while you burn. And don't play innocent with me, Mr. Elvis impersonator, Miss "Queen of Pop"...

Your homilies and homespun da da do. Democracy as will of god, and what a god! Great Lord Nasty Sky. Big Mr. Hegemon. Suffocating, toxic. Bebop-a-loola, be my baby; the sick, sordid details, the 'me so horny' and all that...

To crucify Oscar Wilde was bad enough, but to clone him? Your bumbling genetic "research" (guilt perhaps?), a step too far...

My calling-card prominent on the escritoire of Henry James, supper-prattle virtuoso; connoisseur of twenty-year old port and nineteen-year-old boys.

Your filth, but no smoking; drink and dine, make merry, but don't drive home: "stay a while for cakes and coffee," or "peanut-butter-cups and fat-free milk," or what-have-you...

Oh, brutal you! Brutal you! Passive, plodding, inert at the extremes of pain and fear.

I'm so damn sick of you. I loathe you. I've never known you, you mustn't be. You aren't but the ashes of my cigarette, heaping, as I sip my coffee and look longingly to Spring, but instead see you, you, only you: The Future. Devolution and extinction of my world.

News and Improved: Rumors of Extinction Greatly Exaggerated

Nuclear minds spin atavistic myths grown heavy through chain reaction and accretion. You know, like: "Giants lived in those days. Better, stronger, fitter, smarter, aesthetically superior by orders of magnitude," and so on.

The panicked masses hungered for sacrifice. Threw Miss Liberty from yon high government steeple so that "icons of the steeple, by the steeple, for the steeple shall not perish until birth." Or live lives, however brief, bereft of consequence.

No compromise is possible or desirable within our System of Punishment. Government. Decay.

We heard the buzz. Word gets 'round. We busted the whole hive, even those who named names. We took photographs, confiscated weapons -- unregistered stingers, bio-weapons (allergen-packed pollen and the like).

Snitch for snatch. A Songbird. Siren is the weather vane just like her mother. Cold, not fair.

Full hive (after the mysterious disappearance of The Queen) producing round the clock for HoneyCo Distributors, Inc., "employer" of numerous agents. Eyes and ears in every cell and crevice of their wired hive.

New. Improved. Pure. Natural. Organic. Against Animal Cruelty. Clear, clover honey and other sticky sweets. More and better stuff to come, plus shipping and handling.

Coming soon: The Green Menace. Over-population of frogs. Invasion of amphibious marauders. Bring your bat and gunnysack. They make good eatin' and goddamn it if they aren't multiplying out of control....

Do your duty. Be alert.

Between Nothing and Forever

Even as a kid it was a question of Death. Death, or motion, speed. On the swing-set, flying high, like in adulthood, he'd be running. Swinging for life, yet more life, another century of life, life, on its way and still to come, yes more life coming.

He sang:

"I'm gonna live to be a-hundred-and-seven-years-old!
I'm gonna live be a-hundred-and-seven-years-old!
I'm gonna live to be a-hundred-and-seven-years-old!"

But why so terrorized at seven years of age? Why obsessed to the point of ritual-thinking?

He was the youngest at the picnic, seven years closer to Nothing than the adult picnickers, all in their twenties and thirties, too far from Beginning-from-Nothing to remember, and even further – most believed – from Forever-After to be awed by the Nothing eternally to come.

He chimed his ditty (prayer?), swinging rhythmically with metronome precision, fifty forward, fifty back:

"I'm going to be a-hundred-and-seven-years-old!
I'm going to be a-hundred-and-seven-years-old!
I'm going to be a-hundred-and-seven-years-old!"

Pendulous. Hypnotic. Doomed.

Big Bang

IT from darkness nothingness imagined gas light heat light and

Bang!

Expanding matter light cools dust rock stars

Bang!

Lightening zaps amoeba soup shiver of sex charge

Bang!

Hominids crush coconuts with crude stone tools

Bang!

I, Me, Mine It-men becoming thinking

Bang!

Pharaohs, Caesars, Presidents…cannot exist as brutes with brute desires and IT's imagination of eternal light and SELF without courting extinction, on and on and on amen.

Bang!

Power of synthetic suns unleashed by I-Me-Mine It-men. Visions of IT, "in the form of man" made them insane. Believe IT will save them all, revive Yesterday's creatures, buried in the henceforth and pretense, resurrect meat-matter long dead gone.

Hush!

Silence over deepest darkness nothingness IT moves forever conscious of ITs on and on

Sang Body Electric

In distant memory:

Flash – aural rush of Candy-O; spark shock neural circuits.

Nothing solid to hold, we know too much about what we are and how we know, but you know the necessity of keeping your own history intact, that is not to lose yourself to sun and moon and some kind of Mexican, not tamales, fajitas, cult objects, I don't know, some trip through the years, long time ago, digested and disposed.

"Too serious" abounds and can't be, that is, serious, if it's not eternal, what we try to contemplate, from the comfort of green chairs, the eternal we believe is in us but we know cannot be, simply because of what we think we know.

Perhaps not we ourselves but ones who know and write books about the faces from Africa, Mexico, Egypt timeless in our dreams, perhaps we ourselves not only not timeless, not even ourselves, but minerals, chemicals, fibers, sparks intangible, but with enough R&D they'll find out what it is, and cruel bastards that they are, tell us.

Sure it was better to believe that to be human was to be next to godlike, and even after we killed god, well, that was okay too, because then we were better than next to godlike, we were gods, but the Ones Who Know caught up to us and you can't blame them, for how else will they sell their pills?

Don't get me wrong, I believe, I believe the pills work to make us some kind of happy, but I'm merely suggesting that maybe depression was not so bad if we were at least ourselves and not whatever it is they'll ultimately find out we are when they consult their books.

And don't blame Darwin for this, he merely noticed we evolved, and wasn't it good that at first we were less than what we are and then we became more?

But now we are, well it doesn't matter really, whether we are less or more or even if we become, because it can all be broken down and mapped in formulas and code and what not, like the "first loves" whose immutable memories we cherish were – even at the time – chemicals, hormones working mojo on our pineal blah,blah,blah, cerebral bleh, bleh, bleh in loco pubis orgasmus of flagrant delicto, and so on and so

That's why we drove the nice car to the restaurant so later we could go to the back seat, and now — years later — the love is not even a memory we own but electricity working the synapses and whatever to stimulate the thing-a-ma-jig and bring the whole scene to light, embellished, mind you, by daemon of imagination, and passed to consciousness. In other words our yearn, yearn, yearn amounts to nothing.

Not even the pain of aeon's slaughter, quashed desire, and minds lost on a billion killing fields and deathbeds can be — what? rationalized? justified? — if the lover beside us, our currently significant other, is not even an "other" (naked ape), but an organic-machine-orgasmic. Yes, he/she, from ideal first love to final "one and only truly," all of them, complex systems, organized (by what who when where how?) compendiums of pure *stuff*.

We interact in the big systemic hierarchy, make it our "drama." How we march through the day-to-day without choking and puking is a mystery, perhaps one of the few mysteries left for us common folk who live instructed by the cemetery's narratives, animated by the chemical-spark that drives us through eras to do what we do and cherish what we believe, are told and expected to believe is good and sacred.

I see shadow-figures on the edge of all this, I see neurons, I see the end of trying to fathom wherefore or why, the end of pleasure and pain, cause even if we feel what we feel we know we are not feeling it, for we are no longer ourselves, it's just energy coursing through the system in response to stimuli, signifiers significant of semiotic something or other …

We use symbols of … we term it all "I" or "we" or "us" for reference … language, abstraction, blah, blah, blah, bleh, bleh, bleh … easier to name things, whether they mean anything, that is are important, or not, for all grammars grammar requires nouns.

I'm so sad and disappointed, but I'm not really, because I AM not, really, and there are ones who can prove this and ultimately will, after the proper research, and publish it as fact and make us curse their names for stranding us between two worlds: that of the spirited, eternal "who" and the sensual but senseless "what…"

Carbon

Indeed it will be "transformed utterly, utterly transformed," terrible but sure no beauty.

Rocks, trees, grainy amber waves grisly as Mother, six feet under. Momma! Momma! Carbon. I remember her warm. I knew her as skin.

Like I recall that that car I'd saved pennies (shiny money melts like snowflakes on a stove) to possess; like I recall my high-school sweet-heart's teenage girls; my sultry wife; the color flash color-bled, counterfeit fire-flowers that (over)exposed it all to Krishna's unfathomable *kisser* like ten thousand suns.

Same old, same old: idiots with matches playing god created all this sudden empty, silent breathless, burnt black Dawn. The Sun also rises, still, yet, again, concealed by heavy metal clouds, a leaden pall, warped woof of ash.

Hands wove this. Hands of men who have no hands human eyes might know. Transformed utterly, utterly transformed ... to greasy turds of coal; the world a big burnt marshmallow tongued by concupiscent cosmic flame.

So, spit on the ashes. Douse your white-hot rocks. Enjoy this morning-after life of cold, soot, mud.

Clock Speed

Once, I could barely walk. I lived like a vampire, off strangers' blood.

Too much suck, my hard-drive brimmed. Before I'd grepped to glean, sort, sift, digest; before I could process and make clean, it was gone, all of it, extinct: memories of Life and Love distant as stars.

If data travels at electric speed (so long as servers hum like clock-work: cleaned, tuned, Enlightened) what effect on works and days, and other presumptions of this, the Sixth Extinction?

One day, new beings will evolve, perhaps from flies, a thousand eyes for every buzzing brain; incessant flight from this gross pile to that, no time to dream of dreaming.

Nothing at all.

Cocaine Sonata

I remember radiance. Music. Dance (I know, I know: captive culture; lap dog eyes; idiots mugging for cameras and what not) but re-memory refers to days when I was bright, the music deep, and every dance a super nova potpourri snap flash-on-flash-off of shoes glass phosphorescence and cocaine.

Thumping bass rhythms in starlight and "forever."

Before life turned graveyard there were trees beyond the stones. And grass, and flowers, our backs wet with dew after the dance, after the rut. We lay for hours listening to moonlight, young enough for such amazements without shatter or reproach. And not a moment's email or "remorse."

I remember, I imagine. I recall

Cult Wired Hard

America, civilized, cult wired hard. Urban Uranium Ur. See plus-plus, sea town of Gloucester. Hardwired Olson. Creeley wired hard. Mainly framed, mocking programmers' sea pearl of "mythic child-spray" said Creeley. Olson added, "Misty surge hormonal."

Energy. Silicon. Ur-Mind. 3-D action sound in digi-decibel diffusion. See: video. Digital. Video. Yet hopelessly linear "on faith."

Blank. Blank. Blank.

We were elegant in our sins, and casually dressed. Time happened, and there was no escape, not even to The Word.

An old woman lost her balance in the pharmacy and fell, twice.

Are you all right?

Certainly. Today I'm writing the President. We can't go on like this forever. Not another day like this, in fact. We can't go on.

Walking in time to the rhythm of madness, less burdened dead than alive, I too am writing the President, in a language other than our own.

Ode to Cupid, Psyche, Herb

Cupid, lean, mean, boyish, but no brat, nor heavenly bun of baby fat, plunged wild-eyed into Psyche (lissome, fragrant, amber-thighed; like ripe, exotic fruit – denied).

Clever, subtle boy, at ease in darkness, wet with joy, his tongue danced dithyrambs the gods alone can hear, and some women in dreams, when youth is near.

This long night, seasoned like years, this holiday from boredom, fear, was sliced like salmon skin by ice-blue lights -- flash! flash! and shrill metallic screams of sexless sirens. Punishment for pleasure pursued prior to Law's blessing.

Psyche was seventeen and Cupid timeless, immortal, though, seemingly, a boy at time of coitus (interuptus). Neither would submit to celibacy, not for yet another Spring. Flowers in bloom, potent weed, wine, music -- oldies from Golden Times, sung by a lean electric Orpheus. Would they really bust Psyche for "corrupting" the young god? or vice versa, ad nauseum, infinitum, and a closed loop of etceteras?

LAW, blunt of brain but sharp of ear, in order "to make things perfectly clear" presented Cupid Caught before his mother, Venus, and delivered Psyche unto her Daddy, Herb. Though The Man crashed Psyche's night, must everyone denounce Delight (to responsible authorities, of course)?

Venus, great of girth, no longer Love's bright star, spent seven minutes in the back-seat of Herb's car. She would, of course, have gone on longer, but LAW again proved crueler, stronger: Police of Fate, not Men, were now to blame that Herb, drunk, useless, prematurely

... came.

To be fair, Herb has a story of his own. He is a man. A human being, Mortal, American, in a body past its prime. Nothing prepared him for the swift passings that brought him here, to the night of Psyche's (and her mother's) disappointment, in back of a car he himself had driven with confidence, once, long before Psyche was a glimmer in Olympian eyes. This was not his night, his story. He'd been at home, drinking beer, watching television, dwelling on the past.

He asked for none of this. He did not want it.

"You had no right to raise me from the dead," Herb, unto the heavens, said.

"We can do anything we want -- so long as it's fun," said the god of gods, Jive. "We provide, and LAW taketh away. We gave you your years."

"And LAW took them away. Give me more," demanded Herb. "I want more years -- good ones. A refund, as it were."

But Jive showed Herb his broad back, wide and hard as Texas, and moved on to the next unhappy caller.

"Thank you for choosing Olympus as your Holy Site of choice. This is Jive, god of gods. It's so good to hear from you. Please note that this conversation may be monitored for purposes of quality control, to help us serve you better. How can I help you today?"

"I want...I need..."

"Your call is very important to us. Please stay on the line."

And Jive pushed the red button, "hold," and went out for pizza and "domestic" beer, or perhaps burgers and "imported." Whatever. Who knows? The ways of gods and LAW are queer, cruel, mysterious and cold.

Déja Vu Again

Returned too far again. Life too short again, range so thin. Trying next week-month-year – like poking quanta with a spear. I mean the range is thin.

I entered Beginning blank, deep to my neck in Mother. She squeezed like a python to constrict me to the years. From dawn to Time Machine. Blind repetition.

Work-a-day-mud-walk-a-day, like everyone else. I lived and lived (and living, lived live, in real-time) not knowing or remembering to change a thing. Second-by-second, hand-to-hand, day-by-day-by-day-by-build The Machine and enter to recall. To try, try, try to recall.

But it's too late, again, I'd set coordinates, traveled Time Speed back to first Light. Wretched – again – again foul coordinates, and again, "only yesterday" eons ago. "Again again" begs the question: Does life begin, or end, or neither? Are we locked in a loop of infinite recursion, futile Zero of snake-eat-tail, thou blasphemous Machine?

Depart From Consume

TheyThemTheirs would have us believe we'll never, not properly, die, unless and until They let us, properly, depart forever from ever. Depart from consume: wear and tear unbreakable "goods;" gobble lies, unpunished by deracinators of Real Noire detection: natural, relentless, perishable gumshoes, mortally sensitive to light, air, sound. We fear Death. We fear energies that liberate.

Entertainment. The spectacle of Revolution. Such things as dreams are made on, and public executions. Death be not loud, or factory pour faire de cushioned "cross-train" sporting shoe, say slaves of The World; buzz labor bees; yawn tired wretched huddled massive yearnings to sting clean.

Sing or serve: Sing for your supper, or serve it to an Other: pray this Other lives kind, merciful moments and tips large to sustain. Sustain, that you may sing and serve again.

Sing, sing a song, or serve.

Death and The Academy. Might of Institutions spawn exceptional "tendencies." Bare legacies bear inquest. Submit to the eternal serve. Forever lesser will, will forever lesser evil, evil serve?

Nevermore, nevermore, nevermore. Life -- Theirs, not Ours. Theirs to poke, prod, play. Technical toys of idiot children, delicate dolls, loved so desperately they're soon despised, devoured, "disappeared." Wept over at meal-time, nap-time, bedtime, sweaty, sleepless night.

Heaping helpings of forever bring forgetfulness and sleep. Oblivious awakening to imbecilic laughter: something, something, or nothing repeatable at all.

So, left behind with heaps and mounds of childish things, we grow impatient living, and greater becomes the possibility that Death is real. We find ourselves compassionate, and more forgiving than They taught us was possible. We learn to know more ways of Life than Death.

We live in realms not yet conceived. Imagination, our capacity to know, if They would only leave us alone with their "self evident," common-sense "wisdom" enforced by Law, advertisement, rhetoric, repetition, surround sound video hypnosis, and let us negotiate our "Truth" properly defined, attained, constructed according to exploration, observation, (no certainty but in possibility)!

Such a "truth" without fine-print; loop-holes; paperwork; or other bureaucratic hoc-us-pocus; sinister plots, cunningly designed; artfully placed traps, detours and entanglements. Such a truth, properly defined, might finally, actually, profoundly, without sentimental artifice or self-consciously "hip" sarcasm, distance, cool, etcetera, etcetera, etcetera, such a truth might really "set us free."

Desert Law and Write-Ins

Papers arrived: The Law. Prose of imperative be-ribboned in fey grammar. Trickle-down discourse barked in the language of command; written, copied, distributed as far and wide as the global jurisdiction of Their rockets. Even the same old same is not the same.

Watch the News. See Their SWAT teams bust erstwhile "hard-working, law-abiding" citizens -- who *still* assume, poor saps, that as "citizens" crammed into the warped belly of this Trojan Horse, they're "entitled" to some godforsaken damn thing or other -- America! America! America! (said with a straight face). Shoot 'em and abuse 'em unto madness. "Of thee I sing." Meanwhile, folks on the wrong end of the screen seek sin without consequence.

Jim and Susie on the front lawn sip warm backwash of last night's beers. What a blast it had been, block party, Night Raid Entertainment provided by the Sheriff and his posse (legally deputized; tipped generously) who busted down a "neighbor's" door in search of weapons, literature, narcotics (not-so-secret shibboleths for "You are vulnerable to whatever we nail you for, whatever sticks, whatever satisfies").

The working men grow restless. So damned hungry, famished, for hot blood, pussy, power over those blind to the loveliness of Paradise, those who light not candles, yet blaspheme the night. "Sprinklers for every half-acre of lush desert lawn are a shameful waste of water," those molly-coddled milksops claim to cameras all over Town.

(but smell the sweetness of the cut-grass blades!)

Gotta be sweet or it's just bad, really bad, all the way bad, puke-piss temple of soupy night and hard turf darkness down as your daughter's misery index bad (lonesome as Coyote reading Gertrude Stein by light of campfire and smog-blurred moon...), that kind of real bad, bad.

Coyote howled: "I ain't interested in nuclear infamies of kings, but low watt, barely audible frustrations mumbled day-to-day by numb fragments of history, like you, like me, bequeathed (by what? by who?) three-score years and ten, more or less, of thought, memory, consciousness in Time, of what it meant, then, and what it means, now, to be so finitely aware --"

-- before The Posse shot Coyote dead and left him cold. A token offering, to inky vulture capitalists circling the gray-black dome of Heaven like Rorschach ghouls.

Dreams Like Memories

Hot.

Sky blue green bloom warm beautiful.

Bright shining networks of machines within. Air-conditioned cool as autumn.

He broke the Internet, he feared.

Is your machine plugged in? Did you try plugging in your machine? asked the Help Desk.

Oh. Yes. Of course. How embarrassing.

Nothing to be ashamed of. People 'break the Internet' all the time.

"Something trivial as a misplaced symbol might cause the program to behave very differently."

Very differently indeed. Irrational. Don't pause to think. Enough about them. How are you?

Working hard. Late nights, coffee, occasionally speed. Low-level amphetamines. Nothing serious.

The reunion in May. Dreams like memories.

She died of—?

Brain Cancer.

How sad. Not old. Not old at all. Quite young, in fact.

Forty-six. Only thirty-six when we knew her. To us, that was old.

We were impossibly young.

(She, still dead, appears on stage. Old, thrift-store clothes, granny glasses, long wild hair)

"Heard melodies are sweet, but those unheard are sweeter…"

I hear her voice as if we are there, right now, THEN.

System meltdown. Can't move my arms.

The cafeteria is empty!

No one in the Main Office. The machines are idle. Bright lights and silence.

That horrible day of tragedy and loss. Unjustified. Relentless.

Never so alone, not even in dreams.

"Beauty is youth, youth, beauty..."

Freudian slip into mythical-magical mangled syntax; the hysterical Unknown.

Nothing satisfied our expectations. Nostalgia is fear of and for the future. Nostalgia is knowing you survived. You made it through intact. The Past has always been the safest place to hide.

Beautiful bodies come and go. Energy, desire. All of it grows old.

...all we ever meant to locate...

I don't understand.

Listen. I say, hey diddle, diddle, the Spacemen fiddle, a goose-stepped over the moon.

Yawn yawn yawn, the girl behind her.

Listen. Sol is not eternal. Matter does not matter, little girl, little girl.

I don't want to hear that. It's depressing.

May I be excused from Life? I have to use the bathroom.

Why have the phones stopped ringing?

My phone rings.

Don't interrupt.

May I please be abused? I mean, "excused?"

Listen. Time when, time was when ...

Time is a rocket.

Time made us numb.

"Time present exists in time past" Never understood what that meant, still don't. Just see Time as time for the times-of-our-days. How quickly they pass.

Moments cast velveteen shadows. Holes in the sky leak toxins. The Emperor of Ice-cream has no clothes.

Once we were in season. We ripen, rot. Fish float belly-up. Sky-scrapers' reflections slice The Mall. The gods grow bored with our transactions. No time for refrigerators. The children have no teeth. The Killer's count-down. The death-march.

They creep into your code unnoticed. Sickening. Repulsive. Real pain in the ass too. They take forever to get rid of.

More and more the bottomless empty, but take along that talisman, might do you well. After all, in a world gone mad, the sane are freaks.

I sing of Liberty, such a pretty young thing, I pray for her rescue – bear with me now – from those bloated people and their cigarettes! But Friday we get paid. Something, something must be done. Money doesn't fall from Heaven. That is, one needs to think. To plan. To cogitate.

The Unforeseen can introduce itself to any moment.

We recalled nothing but her darkness, her clock radio, her sad smile. The little things. Her phone number and street address.

Earth Day

Oh thou Guerrilla-hearted, monkey-souled marauders! Slaves! Recycle your abortions, more numerous than beer cans, condoms, candy-wrappers, like leaves in grass.

Oh asphalt jungle children of phosphorous rocket-birds and napalm-spitting insects. Oh top gun predators like razors ripping sky-blue sky. Oh bombers shitting poison apples over Snow White's virgin girl.

Oh groupies of Knowledge with your puerile faith in "Them," that "They'll figure out – something."

"They," of course, already have.

We were all so smart and fashionable. So technical, liberal and "free." Oh to be dumb again and naked. You can pursue Life, Liberty and Happiness, or you can be civilized. You can't have both.

The Tree of Knowledge was the first razed by the Land-Lord's loggers. Great gob, splattering beast blood, marked Life next for lumber.

Ectomorph

He majored in Business, if I recall.

Worked two jobs, one flipping meat-pucks at "MacDonald's," the other doing god-knows-what for tenured professors in the Faculty Lounge.

Work-study, working class, work work work.

Body builder man of steel. He pumped iron. Church on Sunday. Brawny-bulky, awkward in suits. No "believer," really. He followed the regimen Mother, instilled in him when he was – the ritual – you know how when you…whatever, you do your duty, save your soul, try not to think. So soon it's done. The people leave. He volunteers to…to do, to do, to do.

He lacked the raw gut cruelty to "make it;" he was destined to work hard. Not smart, but hard. Live a life of health, cleanliness, grim good cheer.

Despite the cunning orifice that opened him in dreams.

He hated, feared, despised the night, yeah, blessed be the Early Bird clock-radio-alarm metallic dawn chirp summoning to work:

Command type print; type print command; print type print. Command. Command. Command.

Finally the evening work-out: run push lift stretch fart inhale exhale.

Night came soon and often.

Night swallowed him whole endlessly, so deep he trained himself – discipline, discipline – to know and acknowledge "this is a dream, only a dream, I will wake to work eventually, soon, like…NOW!"

Bob to the surface of consciousness gasping like a diver up for air. Rigid. Startled (scared, actually, scared shit-less). Pajamas soaked with sweat, urine; his wife curled fetal on her side.

Oh yes, he had a wife: stylish, vague; spooked by his "episodes", never failed to panic; but she stayed, (for he was a decent man, a gentle man, built like Achilles, though always tired, tired – well no wonder, working hard the way he did!)

Escaped, again. Always he escaped again.

But one Night — fate, inevitable; slow violence of Time — he'll lose the will, the speed, the discipline, to surface before — ECTOMORPH, filthy, degenerate phantom (black teeth, mummy lips, long, cracked, nicotine nails) takes him down. Deep dive down. Merciless.

And worse: calls him back again, back back again, to decadent descent, to the curse and finality of Memory and Sleep.

End Day Kiss

I

"Blow away dark clouds of war!" the schoolgirls sang.

Uniformed, strategically nubile, baring skin, they hop-skipped off to market.

A Scotch Bonnet pepper burst over Tokyo with the power of a thousand suns. Scorched their tomorrows (rhymes with sorrows). Mega-Scoville-unit flash of Hiroshima torn of age, of Nagasaki Lords of Heat and Light, of barbeque, barbeque (white hot singe yer tongue).

II

Oh, burnt marshmallow eyes! Oh scattered ashes that were you...

Saved G.I. Joe from "poof!" and downed your rising sun rise (poof!). Uncle Sam – Sammy! Sammy! Sammy! – will take you all on (poof!), one at a time it's only fair (poof!), like Young Abe Lincoln threw Jack Armstrong (oomph!) and his scruffy gang of rowdy ruffian rapscallions, who despite scars, "kills" notched on wooden legs, bad teeth, severe post-nasal drip, had – every one of them had – hearts of gold.

III

Sirs,

As a tax-paying citizen I demand a "direct hit," specifically to the brain or other sub-system vital to the perpetuation of my person; however, if such terms cannot be arranged, a box seat within radius of ground zero will suffice. I refuse to be caught outside the Box, the Zone, the Zero, the Mark. Pain, acute pain more than I have ever known, is wisdom I would prefer not to acquire.

So, just one thing I ask of you (just one thing, Sugaree): place me within bull's eye distance of the blast. I'll wear a crimson top-hat and green jumper with red fluorescent target, front and back, declaring my coordinates (you can't miss me).

Sincerely,

A.S.E.

IV

I remember seasons before End Day, guest of every thatched hut, crash-pad, art deco den of inequity that warmed the globe. I remember End Day like family, hungry company, dressed casual as Summer.

"Long as you feed him he won't leave," the Old Folks warned.

Naked at night (and tatooed!), good ol' End Day helped himself to thatched hut, crash-pad, art deco family victuals. End Day casual as Summer.

"Long as you feed him he won't leave."

Naked as day, at night (and tatooed!), End Day bid "Good-bye" to cotton casual, khakis, denim, bride white flannels.

"Hello" gross, puckered folds of blood-stained birthday-suit of End Day.

End Day, raider of Frigidaires, burgler of dreams, morphed to such nightmares as schemes are made on, and sold to suckers as sparkling vistas, pristine visions, or heaped upon the poor:

"Here's your slice of the pie, kiddo. Enjoy! But be thrifty. Save. Don't gulp it down at once you'll get a belly-ache, you'll wake up in the morning with a belly-ache and nothing."

V

Oh, what a beautiful morning: so much bird-song, greenery, flowers. Shame it all must burn.

What day End Day say to cower in our cellars? Tuesday, was it? All supposed to disappear next Tuesday. Thunder-flash and poof! Ashes to ashes. Dust. Vapor. Planetary dry-heaves and a cough of sputum goo. All over before crying can commence. Too quick to even scream.

"Don't feel bad," End Day told us. "Think of the hopes and wonderments of Beginning. Think of ice-cream and the casual promises of New Time. Think of a covenant between persons, individuals, young people, free people, in love. Think how it will feel, the taste and scent of raw desire, anticipation for the everything and the all-at-once and the more, more, more, End-day!"

Like a kiss.

Goodbye Alaska

His secretary bought the ticket to Alaska, dropped it on his desk in earnest, left him simmering in oils of nightmare. A series of blunders led to this predicament.

Alaska is disintegrating. The natives' earnest efforts to make perma-frost stay stuck, a geological nightmare, did nil to amend their predicament, and Nanook, nabbed hording snow, received a ticket.

He awoke from a nightmare in which a series of missteps led him to Alaska where the trees and polar bears are dying and earnest Eskimos, their igloos soft as sorbet, pray for one-way tickets the-hell-outta the White Man's petroleum predicament.

The ticket in his pocket read "First In His Class, Seat A," but he didn't need it after all: his predicament was solved when Alaska floated straight to him. True, it was a nightmare for dedicated sunbathers, but to be earnest, "life's a beach (full of Alaska)."

Home Entertainment

History, all fifteen minutes (or is that Fame? two nuts from the same tree), came unannounced, to Town.

History's tree, knotted, leafless, at the Home Entertainment Center (sign above reads "Do Not Enter"), "Chapel of anguish and dismay," according to Grandma and her diabetic cat.

Save the screens, batten the door. If you've the cash, lay down traps, mines, grenades, lest "The Chapel" regain its reputation as a tiny nook of horror, where doors slide at will; falling books smash laptops into bitty bytes; searing sun-rays shuck pearls of code from laser-bitten discs, resurrected from light's smoldering ember (like old songs made new, when first remembered); after-emissions of ghostly tantrums; spiced decay of children's rooms – often the child, so unexpectedly deprived of breath, takes years to learn she can't simply "go home" from death (the heat the heat down there, it's murder for mere spirit to withstand and ghost on not-living).

Children relive their brief, sad biographies on flat digital screens. Desultory mouse-clicks summon blockbusters home: horror, romance, comedic shtick; every genre's "important" contribution to TV renderings of tumid books, where prudery and sighs em-purple every page, hallmarks of "Victoria's" reign, when every writer, laureate or runt, agreed: a pretty face must never own a c—; and mounds of fabric, hiding pokes, were common among many tropes these "classic" authors used throughout their tomes to render them Christian in the privacy of private homes.

No one, whether on a goof or dare, thrill or pledge, visits The Chapel alone; certainly not after dark, haunted as it is by giggling gamin Ghosts: naked girls and wild-haired boys consort with photon phantoms of the silent screen.

The most frightening, tragic, scene was the apparition of a queen—of film—caressing a creepy girl of fourteen or fifteen, who shared a similar birth date—day and month, not year, and here's something to ponder: the girl was "Native," of the wild.

But every so often life will catch us by surprise, and from our bedroom floors real spirits rise to warn us we're not really all that nice, that everything we own is soaked in blood. There are even some, among the jealous, un-American and un-free, who claim a drum is beating always, though we can't hear it with our scientific ears, heralding the worst of our fears: that soon will come a time we'll cease to be, and even ghosts with all their histories respond to Fate's imperious command with ectoplasmic tears, for much as they've reason to despise us for our mockery of every sacred place they'd known and all the lies burnt into Entertainment Center discs, and libel in our flashy coffee-table histories. Because we feel not hence fear not – for our selves or our own, they pity us. Centuries of loathing melt to air when they see how deep yet meaningless is our despair. They'll watch us die like rodents drowned in wet cement; impervious to death as life; oblivious of "now" and "real"; caring only that "this" (the present, the Now) is not like that horrendous dream (or was it film?) of being stuck inside with spouse and kids and *nothing* on the screen.

Immortal Fictions

When I read "To Constantia Singing," I dreamed of Constantia singing. Summer of 1816, the one Big Media reanimates in sentimental films. I read the Summer of 1816, when I was sixteen, Summer of 1981, dreaming future reading past.

Shelley, Byron. Open collars and wind-blown hair. Sex, drugs, guitars and "vintage" psychedelic garb a century and a half before The Beatles.

Summer, 1816, it rained and rained. Mary, Percy, Claire, George and creepy Pollidori enchanted each other with horror stories they would leave for goofy posterity to bastardize on big and little screens.

Young poets alive with life. But also ugliness. Accusations. Dead and stillborn children. Claire's womb infused with madness. Scion of the Lord.

I suppose it was a "youth movement" of sorts – certainly Piccadilly and the Haight inherited their style. But it was all just talk. Conversations in the parlor and on the lake. Julian and Maddolo. White Anglo Atheists. Percy's pressure to perform, to walk in visions of poesy, out-pace the game-legged Superstar.

The boat, the lake, harbingers of – well, one should learn to tread water if drawn to it.

Laudanum, pistols, Greek and Latin chit-chat; aristocratic irony; impassioned bookish banter.

Could they have foreseen Karloff and and American kids in flat-head masks on Halloween, before the monster was a grunting imbecile incapable of polyglot discourse?

I saw a lock of Mary's hair encased in glass the Summer of 1990 at the New York Public Library, some ghoulish exhibit come to edify the young. The hair was light-brown, flecked with gold. Honestly, it could have been clipped from any teenage girl "just yesterday."

But it was old. Older than the rubber mask I've kept since I was six.

Note: monster mask, not "Frankenstein Mask," as the label advertised. Frankenstein was not the monster, but the Muse.

That is, before incorporated, at a later date, into the fiduciary corpus, and brought, legally, to life. Immortal fiction, walking, talking, killing, eating. Miraculous necromancy. Mobilization and manipulation of a million lifeless parts. Human once – the pieces, the parts – once infants at the breast.

Less Than

In the dream time long ago ....

Cosmos coughed galactic stardust formed life, mind. Celebrated human stardust in the console: virtual teletype screens simulated terminals eterm, aterm, xterm fixed width font ISO-8859 in color "everybody has one."

"Well I won't say it, but it rhymes with rocks and runts (tee-hee tee-hee, chucklechuckle, chucklechuckle, tee-hee tee-hee, chucklechucle chucklechuckle)."

"Believe me I can help you if you'd only let me in…"

"Not by the hair of my botox chin quim."

Note: the medium is not the message, the medium is just a box. The message is ashes to ashes to dust to self-loathing not for failing to "become" society, to "measure up;" failure to beat its clock; failure to find freedom and an "out." Faiure to GET OUT from under Panopticon vistas of THE MAN in the Moon (and everyplace else).

Wave His flags, die for His dreams, fight His wars, wretched creatures, His domain, creatures of habit, ritual, autistic, doomed…

Mumford, page one of "Technics and Civilization" says we are less than, says we are nothing more than semi-rational components of The Machine and damned if he ain't on to somethin' …

Was on to something. He wrote that in '67, hard-cover first edition beside your "Doors" and "Sargent Pepper," (maybe Otis Redding) in the station-wagon/van TIME dubbed "Summer of love," draft card in your pocket, California dreamin' of mega-technics and the demigods who love them.

Suckers. Where is your Chicago Seven now?

Mannish Eyes

"Young adult" at eighteen, resident of Father's home, matured admirably to twenty.

At forty I turned twenty-one, not that it mattered, for they were dead, all of them, the ones to impress, deceased. The Old Man too. Da. Da. Gone.

Across the ocean, to the shore of my nineteenth year, that Summer of sun, sand, song. Girls young to love – not as daughters, lovers, then, – as lovers then, and wine, and moving toward, looking toward, confident, impatient toward forward, forward, don't look back.

What happened? What? What torsion wrenched the spine of my Time crooked; felled the Smithy of my Soul; stopped all growth emerging at the onset of my going?

My going forth to be out there and do.

The then, then, and then: slow, painful hammering to upright (worked the crippled Smithy). Facing grief, loss, mortality with placid, mannish eyes.

I'd like to call it "wisdom," not "resignation" in defeat, but really I'd rather swim. Back.

Back?

Back, back, yes. Yes. Back – to the forward of my shore.

Commercial Brake

You police me, I'll please you, Fellow Amerrigan, my fellow Amerigo. Grow up to realities of give and get-give: Stiff mechanics of cling-free exchange: market market market, babe, you know? For instance: How much for Momma Pharaoh, Papa Pharaoh, PLUS the dead baby "preserved" in that jar of honey (to be re-interred at a later date with all honors and obsequies befitting a minor mummy—pun intended—and a Museum Ceremony on Live TV, replayed later on The News, maybe a celebrity dance or awards show)?

How much you think they're willing to pay?

It is a museum, after all, with major corporate endowments, and the future is embedded in the past; hence, its preservation. They, the ones who rule, are existentially responsible. You gotta think. Also: "cash up front" or "send in the Marines…"

Not a bad "M.O." according to the newspaper men, an iron fist is worth two guerrillas in the bush, not to mention a boatload of drugs and epigrams invoked at tax season and anything else you get to "sweeten the deal." Come to that point, you're well past anything but meat."

The Museum does look well, but don't push it: a deal is a deal. I got it all in my head, every detail, biography, memo to Pharaoh, every last courtesan's rival's son's mysterious murder.

(The man on the other side of the screen's got Mojo in his lap, know what I'm saying? *Do You Know What I'm Saying?* Don't for a minute think he won't blow you right outta your couch, tater tots and all…)

Don't think at all, in fact, not for a minute. Leave it to The Experts; They've got it under control. All of it. Relax. Feel good about yourself. Do *not* induce vomiting.

That whole situation sapped me too. Sucked me, drained me, stepped on me and squashed me. Sad, sad, sad to think about all They'll lose after They win – and this is the first time I am thinking about it…

Do NOT induce vomiting. We'll be gone soon. Who wants to deal with that kind of mess, on top of everything else?

Our bags are on their way. They'll make it home before we do. They'll be waiting. We're done here.

Great American MEme

MEme is the idea I call myself. Descent Hungarian, Polish, Jewish mating birthing moving dying. Talking, planning, dreaming continuous till death did they part. Sudden alive and young me, new century. Educated in the grand tradition of public schools and television. Calvinist Consumerist American MEme. Media stealth blitz ravishing The Word. Images more potent than, more lively than, more sticky than. Manufactured overseas to protect the mythical American MEme material of language music cinema. MEme the holographic cells of Body Politic. I mourn the loss of me to Me. Duplicitous double-agent Time works for The Myth Machine now; later to replace or simply erase me and leave nothing, silence, void. I remember. I remember me in motion. Doing being and aware of doing being in Time ("what happened?"). Proof of me my self alive and separate from Me Body Politic. Goose-stepping acolyte and yes-MAN Me on loan from Time to Time. THE BODY POLITIC ME equates me with your neighbor's drooling kin in Idaho or Buffalo or anywhere someone somewhere calls "here and now," capitol of work, death, taxes. Citizen Me immortal. Oh poor me (i call myself), the 40 year drama without narrative thrust forward. Primary ME defined by Time, THE MAN, HIS-story. Poor secondary me supine on sunny lawns and beaches of my young. Sentimental dissipation. Scatter, scatter, scatter the mortal earth me of dead skin sunburn to the wild west wind and occasional typhoon. March on, march on, selfless, expendable ME immortal. Billions of me for every ME on earth enables ME murderous to death march MEme. Slaughter devour disperse till nothing left of MEme but ME.

The Mouse of Anarchy

If power is everything and all you want, we can find you a courtier's position consulting the nefarious Man Mouse of imperial Florida's Magic Kingdom; however, you must know your place; look humble, pasty, pale, as if chilled by the ghost Of Walt himself (flash-frozen upon giving up the ghost, for he who lived one life grand was sure to want another; more, at least, than was allotted his humble beginnings: immortality, befitting his position as Divine Majesty of cartoon Kingdom).

Beware the megalomaniac, Man Mouse! He can and will, with the click of a mouse, erase you, file by file, until you're naught but a ghost in the machine. To live safely in the Kingdom and avoid harassment, you'll want to situate yourself in the bland position of cloying, though ineffectually humble, servant. True, the unctuous conniving of the humble is transparent to anyone but the mocking mouse running the show, but regarding your position, who else matters? Surely not that fowl ghost who ducks 'tween tourists, trading sex for access to the Kingdom (true, only a fool would believe anything could get you into The Kingdom but cold cash or credit-card – no – checks – much less sex with a duck).

It is said that he who enters this Mickey Mouse Kingdom through sex, scalping or subterfuge must humble himself before the mercenary Mouseketeers who want lifetime passes to the whole of Mini-Mouse – no ordinary mouse hole – but who stands a ghost of a chance to "get any" so long as the position of MASTER MOUSE remains secure?

To position yourself as a brash usurper of the Kingdom is not only foolish but dangerous, since every ghost in the Haunted Castle, looking for a humble sinecure on Main Street, will rat you to the Mouse, who'll deny you that Duchy you want in Frontier Land (cake position!), where Injuns live free and die of want. But then: even Bambi's ghost might be hard-pressed to humble itself before the Kingdom of that vain, soprano mouse.

A Nostrum for Your Senescence, or Death by Cartoon

1.

Her lavender musk was more like life than poetry or lace.

2.

She sailed through simple trees, drowning in a pool of laughter.

3.

Lunar bird sinks Lethe-ward; bounce back on ACME heels; sustain gun blast to proboscis: smoldering cheeks, no bullet holes or blood: clean as paper for the punch-line: boxer lost to tar-baby: late round knock-out, virtue of exhaustion; such a sticky situation.

4.

Chock full of Chewy Chocolaty Goodness; air-conditioning; a deep couch; cops with attitude; remote control; so many nick-knacks in your living room: how many mirrors do you really need?

5.

"I'm not in denial," she said, wistfully. "This is my next-to-last drink."

6.

Language begets other language: your sentence, wide as the cervix of a whale, yet daintily protective of the loaded egg, streaks like a train between hills, to the place where phrases hide from noise.

7.

this constant taking resigned to tchotchkes stacked chest high recycled with paradigms of Future left behind unpaid for at the counter

8.

Madmen scratch pediments of Banks, Insurance Towers, patina heels of our Immortal Statues oblivious to names printed machine-ically on blank checks, obscure Elysium of heroes, defaced with phone numbers in fat red ink.

9.

Frost is not unusual this time of year; the ground was hard as drum-skin, hard as muscle, hard as ground, yet the Robins managed – thrust-parry-thrust of jackhammer bills – to un-earth breakfast.

10.

"Hurrah for week-ends!" we cheered. "Hurray for the goody goods we have! Especially remote control and night."

Amen.

Perpetual Yearning to Be You

I'll buy you chocolate if you keep me sane. The machines arrive at three o'clock. I'll buy you chocolate if you keep me sane. Celebrities in my head confess secrets, memories, desires only The Elect should know. Consequently common dream-monsters became too shy to charge, creep, terrify or dig.

One night, before the Age of DigiCams, before we lived in cells like bees, I saw a turkey-moose in cirrus cumulus, and a chicken-pot lighted by the moon. Heard German sentences like bull-whips cracking, or small arms fire. Guttural barking at the postman; howling at incendiary Zeppelins; the charred lungs of history, wheezing; the angry protests of Prometheus bound to the Wicked Wild West.

Situation unmanageable. The artist built a cow from scratch. "Okay, do it, but don't be long." Simple enough. I never belong.

All the women in the salon applauded the hair-dresser's performance, though a child audibly muttered, "Must we have meatloaf again?" Mother, our mother, released to the stars. Ashes to ashes. Smoker's cough. Relent. Relax. Rest.

We spoke about prescriptions that help us through the day, and simple moments in the sun, all but impossible in the context of this dying, brown-mottled green.

My drinking buddies inevitably reach false conclusions about work, love, politics – you name it. For instance, did the man in that musical about the phases of the moon drink mead? What the hell is mead? Do any of them even know?

She murdered me years ago but I forgave her, much as one learns to tolerate television's errant decibels.

Insistent waiting for the sentences she came from. Meanwhile, she knew sin to levels unheard of by ones such as ourselves, who daily endure rigors of mortis, without articles, arched ("Hey, I know that tune") to help us through the certainty of what's what and what wasn't, isn't, will never be.

Stop screaming or I'll kill you. Celebrities are out tonight, the sky is clear. Everyone else is suspect – especially suckers of bad air – of trampling the dead. Genetic memories of Yesteryear's hominids, gone but not forgotten. It's an oral culture so we remember what happened. Love. Work. Slaughter ("hey cowboy, that crud under your nails ain't buffalo chips!"). Pain.

What were we talking about? Noise and engines. The chieftain's plume. Incas, Aztecs, NFL football. To even presume inherent value – outrageous. We are but humanoid meat sculpture awaiting completion, revelation, evolution, any ticket to higher levels before it's too late. For all of us.

So he cries "Ego," does he? Let him read the public record.

Sherman Flame and Slaughter

Sherman's march of flame and slaughter. Sherman slash and burn and ruthless, ruthless. "War is Hell," said Sherman, Grant's right arm. Grant and Sherman big cigars glowing like cities left behind in heaps of ash. Sherman's receding hairline, scraggly beard. Lean, tough Sherman inventing Modern Warfare. Scorched earth. Prometheus gave Man fire, which Sherman smeared over Atlanta. Lincoln in Washington and Seward, Stanton, waited for Grant and Sherman, waited for it all to end. Lincoln gangly, dark, obscenely tall. Warm-hearted story-teller, killer. Stanton squat and cold. Abrupt. Means business: these men had work to do. Grant and Sherman's muddy boots; Lincoln and Stanton's musty suits. Orchestrating slaughter to preserve the Union and wage-slavery. Exterminate chattel slavery, the factory's the future runs like clockwork. Low maintenance. Share-croppers. Workers come and go. Input/output. Throughput. Now we live in the Union blood preserved. No such myths as Lincoln, Stanton. No such statues as Grant, Sherman. Once, the Yankees beat the Braves in the world series in four straight games, SLAUGHTERED 'em. I felt heat of Sherman's burning. Atlanta is a different city now, no longer a crucial partner in History 's danse macabre.

Still Life Motor Inn With Prom Queen

She remembered the Before. Before Now hardened to Then; before Life's Autumn of confusion, sadness, lonely drunk wondering. Before the years like shooting stars.

Paula alone at the Inn. Cable television. Spiked coffee. Nicotine. Remote.

Years like shooting stars.

Paul out shopping for mussels and booze. Loose change to call his wife ("business trip and all is well").

Paula by the pool – not quite the season: murk-skin of algae stretched like a cataract across dead water. Insects, rats, frogs, maybe a bird or two suspended in the glop.

Not quite the season.

Paula sits and Paula ponders: how many spiders worth of frog, how many frogs of duck, how many ducks of rabbit bison wolf – step, step, step – steep Ziggurat ascent to talk and code, mutant currency of human be.

Emotional black-market yields inflationary sorrow, sorrow, stark. Value. Her only real, her only own.

"It wasn't a disastrous marriage, merely a failed one."

Her son is eight and with his grandmother who, 20 years ago, had loved Paul like a son.

"I can try to explain," said Paula to and of herself. "But I'd rather not."

Meanwhile, Paul.

Mussels, sauce, snacks: same small-town plaza ("nothing changes"): beer, wine, grenadine, soda, white liquor: "gin-cola, gin-cola, let the boy in, gin-cola, gin cola, I'll love you like sin" – or was it something-something "skin?"

"We are twice the age we were then," Paul said. "The time that's passed between now and then is greater than the sum of our lives – then."

He tossed her several snack-size bags of Crunch Nuggets; the variety pack, 'bursting with flavor.' and colorful designs.

They're thirty-eight. Last time "together" they were eighteen.

Anti-depressants and nicotine gum.

"Nibble me."

See what develops.

"Lotta wrong turns."

"What's done is done."

"God I'm a boozer."

"Talk is stress."

Still Life with Motor Inn. Sun, beach, parking-lot, bushes budding, not yet bloomed.

"Just off the highway."

Talk is stress.

Tiny, barely five feet, and weighed the same she did at seventeen. Paula practiced yoga and foreclosure law.

He'd put on mass. But hadn't lost his sarcasm or hair.

'Class Couple' photo. High School Yearbook face-down on the bed.

"Were we really so special, or just young?" she implored.

"You mean 'our love is the love of loves forever and ever' and all that? It's a belief system, same as any other. A lot more plausible than religion at any rate. Belief systems change. Even if the god-thing or whatever the, the faith, was founded on was – is – true."

Reunion of virgins.

It was Paul's idea to return. To the water; to the motel; to the indifferent long ago.

Still Life with Tentacle

1.

Neither good nor bad, the man on the white horse rode off to Chinese restaurants. Sullen aficionados lost their zest for heroes. The rest went on with their work.

2.

Operators nude over the circuit direct cold calls to /dev/null.

3.

Bodkins of reality carve deep tatoos. The blood is wiped away, like Navajo sand paintings, to reveal runes, glyphs, symbols set in cryptic patterns on bare skin. She lay in bed for days, summoning Death out of the closet with smoke signals from her menthol light. Finally the pain subsided, she was able to obsess over the message, or lack thereof, set permanently between her scapulae and down her spine, stopping just short of the coccis.

Meanwhile, downstairs, Uncle Grissom frightened us with tales of bogeymen and Titans.

"They'll pinch your head, boyo, snap you like a twig, snatch you away…"

Aunt Kim however, was the voice of calm: "Such a shame to invest in your own destruction… sit down a while and breathe…"

"Birds shit on your sleeve get used to it," replied Uncle Grissom.

4.

Alone in his room he ordered Thai food tipped the Thai guy two dollars, masticated, swallowed, stared again into the monitor awaiting signals. When will the Aliens in government black suits deliver his daughter?

5.

Dead writers haunt the shelves of our local library. The local TV newscaster dropped dead on the treadmill in his living-room. He was forty-six, his daughter nineteen.

6.

In the bordello we saw fine lace curtains…an old religioso with a hard-on for god. Noise over the Network summoned us to space. The old woman who lived in the basement where the super had lived – she was his widow? Girlfriend? – she'd been there always or so it seemed. Like he'd been always dead and unable to perform his task. The building was a shambles.

She was unable to open bottles or handle remote controls without assistance from the whores upstairs.

A photograph of her at twenty-two, a "flapper" perched on her peak and ready for thrills.

a. Eat food.
b. Return package.

7.

Mortal, but invincible, outside of time, yet chronically fatigued; symbolic of nothing, devoted to less; money the root of all action; cereal box says it all leads to a balanced life; we used the phased approach.

HE: I'm young yet. There's much to contribute

SHE: I want to kill myself before I die. And fuck grandma's funeral. Spend the money on your kids.

HE: Bright sun with crimson trim…heaven a block away…

8.

They were huge, enormous, and they multiplied…

9.

She was a flower in a black spring jacket.

He had the pinched face of the dog walker.

He shot the moose because it looked at him.

"That's settled then, you can be calm now, you've solved the problem…"

"Oaf, ape, monkey, lout, inarticulate fucking baboon!"

"She looked real nifty in that dress."

10.

She was hot meat; pink sweat and lightening; droll, erotic spider. Shadows of her bedroom burning silhouettes into our skin. Like cloud images. Imaginings. And I don't mean cutesy duckies and horsies in the cumulus but intricate, complex, wild, like fractals. On our flesh. Her bedroom.

11.

Open to narrative suggestion, we unleashed victorious brigades of laughter.

Sum

                                                   "Ah hah! Pronoun trouble."—Daffy Duck

Her father and uncles; later, her brothers, cousins, husband; later still, her sons and grandsons, spilled blood overseas (others' and their own), to defend Our Way of Life.

Of course She had assumed hers was "our" way, the shops, houses, gardens, luncheonettes; Spring parties, Summer picnics, Holiday parades – her town was Our town was Our Way of Life.

When finally Our Way of Life dropped dead, decades-old decrepit shops and "Mom & Pop" eateries were crushed, flattened, kaput. A Super Mall humming with chain stores, and a Factory to manufacture pills, would sprout like bean-stalks from the ruins; the block where she was born and raised, and raised her kids, shall too be razed, the lot black-topped and lined, a carpet for cars of the new work force.

Oh Brave New World of jobs, growth, Free Parking and discount meds!

She told the reporter: "The Courts say we're to receive 'just compensation' for our home. I'm eighty-two-years-old, yet I knew nothing of life's worth until I saw the market value of the only home I'd ever known. The sum. Not a billion dollars, not a million dollars, not anything close. I had imagined…well, what's a lifetime worth? The Developer, the one whose firm owns City Hall – I'm not stupid – said, and he plays hardball, I respect that, he said 'It's not like you're twenty and we're speculating on your future. This is compensation for lives lived. We're actually paying you for time you and your hubby already pissed away. A used house and two used lives. That considered, this is a very reasonable offer…'"

You see, She'd been confused all those years listening and watching: radio, film, tabloid, television Celebrity News Advertise Celebrity Heartbreak Marriage News Indictment Freedom Ingénue Super-Star be Free…

Ever since She was a child, when they sent away the boys from her neighborhood, she'd always assumed it was 'Our way of life' the boys, her boys were killing and dying for, when all along it had been THEIRS.

Their ways, Their lives, Their Eminence and Their Domain.

A life such as hers, or her husband's, or her son's or daughter's or great-grand-daughter's is but a "paltry thing," a dirty napkin on the scale beside Their gold.

Road Puppet Night Core

Twenty years blind dreaming core, where Life is. Dreaming core, where life is.

Now but now but now (But now… but now… but now…) what puppets crouch behind the wheel of this old rig, splintery buttocks propped on books? Whose twig fingers jumped our demo-critical ignition while we dreamed (where life is)?

Never regret those Rip Van Winkle years back of the van, her nectar rain rush – still, but still: this mirthless joy-ride toward that cliff ahead (ahead, see it? Ahead?) seems punishment extreme for merry decades happy, singing (guzzling gaso-nico-techno-lean: kill these killing habits, let it go: crawl crawl; infinity of dream)

Stop this hearse, or I will scream!

Tête de Cinéma

That time she finally agreed:

the future was a movie about life and death and other distant choices. But never anything like this.

Never did tête de cinéma imagine such ineffable, crushing, the, the — down, down, the down, down stacked children. Wounds. Exposed wire. Sores not even worms would pick. Corruption set *before* grenades blasted through lunch, shocked waves of black-shawled crows, the "caw! caw!" of the stricken, the dead falling from trees like stones.

Feathers slick with crude, a saturate burden. Tongue click microphone beat frequencies raise corpses from dyspeptic dreams of Yesterday's News At Eleven.

Bring it on.

Regardless

Not to believe another day could end this way. That we won't finally, after all, wake up. "Just a dream," and all that.

Honestly never imagined it would come so sudden, run-of-the-mill. The process, I mean. The process. Not the thing itself. Unmentionable.

Half naked, damn "gown" won't tie. Cold, steel invasions; over-head television 24/7 (and this is the "good" nightmare, the one with health insurance).

Still believe in Future as a pretense, like "Humanity" or "Democrats," belief for belief's sake, so they don't call you "nihilist" or Gloomy Gus. So "iffy," really; unreliable; so not like we were taught...

Worst of all, it comes – listless, bored, humorless – with Middle-Management-indifference.

Regardless of despair (bottomless), or Nietzschean mastery of faith, or false good cheer; regardless of the utter fictions we lose ourselves to between pills and nurses' "war stories" of meaningless suffering, "we're good people," we tell ourselves, and "we're worth fighting for" – though the fight is against ourselves, something in ourselves...

...and the "girls" who clean our pans and ride the bus, alone, past midnight, really do love us and think about us (alone, past midnight) and want us to get well...

Even when we cover our eyes, put our hands to our ears, scream "Yonk! Yonk! Yonk!" it comes, it comes, regardless of our fear, it comes.

Repetition

Word trauma. Print culture dead after all those years. True, nearly all web pages are mostly print, but talk, written or otherwise, is cheap. Everyone writes, though no one reads the everyones' always writing, no one but themselves at any rate, adding more junk, more artifacts — albeit digital and easily erased — to the proverbial Pile. Screaming raging ranting raving blogging texting worse than television, shut it, I mean shut it, shut, shut the damn thing off. Some, noticeably more than others, are sensitive to the pain of repetition. Honestly Gertrude, I've known "more of the same" but no repetition in rhythm, song, poetry of talk rhythm, sound of life beating, people doing — and of course, talking — people doing Life, even those who deny what Life does to the living, but the dead, who once were living, stay dead and honestly it's no one's fault but their own: they got no rhythm. Life abhors repetition without rhythm: pulse, pump, thrum, like when Injun scouts in movies listen to the ground maybe hear the beating hooves of distant horses, or Hoover vacuum cleaners. Movie rhythms of beating hooves, amplified by orders of magnitude (they're not that loud in real Life actually, loud, but not *that* loud), beating, beating hooves absorbed by earth and amplified by electronic doohickeys (note: check spelling of "doohickeys;" this is not real talk, after all, it is "text"). The dead underground seek rhythm, repetition of the source of the dead instinct to be rid of repetition in the talk talk talk of speech (same old same old) return to rhythm of creation pounding beat toward pump motion, pounding toward no more repeating rhythm (it's all just sex, really, to which most dead persons are indifferent) just simple silence, peaceful, permanent. Oh Death! End of talky talk redundant a-rhythmic repetition and interruption, oh Death, silent as snow.

ROI

Oh explicators and exegetes, define yourselves! May I offer you a nickel?

"ROI," defined as "king" in Frog, (hence legends of The Kiss relived through Kong and Faye; Elvis and Priscilla; Nixon's eyeball licking Jackie's privates as she slept, nude, the drugged sleep of the dead in Aristotle's arms – and John's), expresses "interest," in plain English, Anglo, reg-la-ure Americuhn; "ROI" is a regular expression...

(It began down in the mines, the data mines, mining data, ore of language, raw rock mineral of talk: mine your data, mine your business. Grandiloquent tongue sucker! Ubiquitous maxim-muncher! Possessor and corrupter! Every day another data base another belly-full of jargon; dialect; e-mission creep; techno-beauro-cranymic mad-lib slang of system-think: station house of tropes and babble; "Dead" phrases, still-born remarks. This is Command Central, can you read me – do you want to? Over. Over. [Is-it-finally]Over?

Check out those two agents. Male and Female. Down there at the mine. He in his dark suit, she in her just-as-dark skirt and jacket ensemble. Her high heels; his Oxfords. Their dark glasses.

What can they be up to, pretending to mine data with the balding, overweight poly-syllables. Oddly silent, they don't even take notes. What could they possibly be after? Who ratted us out to the FEDs?

(Repetition: morphemes ripped from glossolaliac wombs, packed onto discs like cattle, flash frozen, carted away...)

It's quite clear, actually, the conspiracy that brought The Agents to this foul place: we are, without acknowledging it, *eating our own words*. But can even these two smoldering detectives – c'mon; they *must* have "done it" at least once; they're over 30 years old for gods' sake – stop this cannibalistic madness before it's too late?

Oh...I don't know. They look kinda faded and worn. Truly I haven't seen them on the job since their show was canceled ten years ago.

They might be a bit out of their league. She never was much of a talker, but He had that dry, confident wit that would certainly be useful down in the mines.

"You're handing in THAT to The Chief?" She squinted from the darkness, darkened further by her shades, which she removed briefly, to let him feast upon the big, wet, life-green planets of her eyes. This made her quite desirable – in a popular detective series kind of way.

"It's all we've got that CAN'T be disproved," He said.

"I just feel like we left something undone. But what could we have done? We were dealing with the innermost complexities of the brain, the very building blocks of mind itself. And it was almost time for lunch," She said, self-consciously flipping her bright red hair to tease Him with her stunning profile.

"I guess we both left our 'participles dangling,'" He quipped, placing his hand awkwardly on her muscular, yet thin and sparrow-like shoulder.

"Speak for yourself," She said, and blushed a wry,'men-will-be-boys' smile…

(ASCII octal numerals in unicode; haunting screams of phonemes muffled by disk-drive hum–; hummmm–; hummmmmmmmmmmmmm–; illusion of free association snared in skeins of code: open the trope, unravel the rope: links to poison applets: you are what you eat, if you can catch it – y'all!)

I mean, you'll pay a dime for the privilege of my nickel; you'll find me interesting, a proper noun of value, an entity worth keeping.

Oh pimps, pushers, peddlers of post-verbal-comic-realism, adulterated weather reports, free radicals and anti-oxidant assassins! May I offer you a Latte?

For if I am here today, and you are here, then my purpose is to serve, yours to consume: else, merry-come-round tomorrow, "collectors," according to Oracles of post-verbal, post-comic, post-poetic bombast, shall congregate with interest:

to make good on promises; to erase uncertainty; to debug every bug that ever crawled the road from Then to Now, when, staggering home from the riotous, heart-breakingly premature celebration of Ascent of Man (and Woman), our sINCESTORS (Adam + Eve + Cain + Able = FamilyOfMan) gazed Heavenward in the approximate direction of The Almighty Father, and said, "You figure it out…"

The Agents duly reported: "Daily we shed unwanted syllables, offal to be studied as artifacts of relative worth, for our interest. If we weren't so damned curious about our own recursive babble, the Data Mines would have shut down long ago. Currently the mines are plumbed for information day and night. It is our considered opinion that we in government, and the tax-payers who bear our burdens, will be stuck with these seemingly bottomless mines for many years to come."

The Ledge

Piper pipe your something like that poem by Blake. US3r sixteen, reading the world, alive to better than, better than, better than he'd known. Possibilities of better magic, now and to come. Clean spines stacked each link in the chain of shopping mall bookstores, unlimited potential to consume – – knowledge – was that what it was? Another consumer scam? Get it all in, get it all now before it's too late and you *miss everything*…

Another family affair. Adult situations. But the kids know all that *parental supervision advised* was not mandatory – can They make it mandatory?

"Pharaoh said we could!"

(stay up late cook Jiffy pop; watch monster flicks – "The Mummy," "Return of the Mummy," Abbot and Costello meet Frankenstein, Dracula the Wolfman, and J. Edgar Hoover")

Pharaoh said we could Pharaoh said" they can do anything because we'll let them paint pretty words, black on white evoking timeless dream-scapes.

Free to vote, protest, speak your mind, run in circles round the block, the indoor track…

The fattest nun of all, Sister Salt-Peter, lost in the folds of her bad habit (black and white evoking timeless dream-scapes), Sister Salt-Peter, celebrity man-killer, sucked into folds of labia thick as slugs.

Turn Century

Watchin' the Detectives nit-pick flaxen locks of Albion. Bad seeds in golden tresses. Tears. Growth unchecked, in unwashed regions, hatch dark unmentionables.

Holmes and Watson combing creepy, misty, filthy streets of London. Watson's trusty revolver in his pocket.

Brittania's oily hair (foggy night, pluck nits and agon; expert sleuth-wit). Bad eggs absorb osmotic protein in the corse of Empire. Night crawlers. Maggots.

Growth in unwashed dark ineffable...

Holmes and Watson scour London, neutralize fire-tides of evil. If only common Heroes knew and understood what Holmes and Watson knew and understood. How deeply they despised the future! Nijinsky. Stravinsky. Houdini knew there would be no escape, not even for the celebrated (Conan Doyle's son lost to Empire's rumble, the War To End All Wars (Until the Next One).

Holmes and Watson door to door like brush salesmen. Contain, control, codify. Wounds-West incurred when Company Men plunged native hearts into despair, PS: the horror the horror.

Watson, Holmes, Freud, Nietzsche, slumped in smoky studies, contemplate Americans on couches eying "COPS."

That is no place for bold men! That is no place for Monk, Columbo, Clousseau, Scooby-Doo bumbling through ritual deduction when the only recourse was force.

Brute Terminator and Lethal Weapons born to Die Hard time and again prove box office morgue receipts...

Heaven collapsed on Marx's head; disciples – rich, famous – stated the obvious: "hell is other people; from this there is no exit; case closed. PS: the horror, the horror etc." New TV Detectives stir WASP nests in Washington, seek answers to rhetorical Arlington and unmarked native graves, pits, tombs.

We're standing on them now.

The Way We Live

My friends are criminals: they smoke pot; they don't eat meat; they or their partners have had abortions, at some point in their lives, or sex with their own sex. They hate war and television, and laugh at mythologies of "heroes" and angry gods who hustle real-estate and issue mad, delirious, homicidal "sons."

They hate the government, the corporations, and anyone who dares call them consumers, not citizens; they hate – but pretend to love; they are civil, obedient, citizens.

My former friends are cowards: they fear "minorities;" they fear government and the terror it sponsors; they "support" Israel and "our" troops for fear that 'it' might happen here, and would rather 'it' happen to Arabs, or "minorities," or anyone but good consumers like themselves who drive big cars and thank god for corporations who – yes "who:" they're individuals under law like you or me, but bring slicker offerings to Christ's birthday than Santa Claus could ever dream.

I met a schoolteacher. Frustrated, frightened.

"All the children are insane," she said. "Most of them. Mad as hatters, immunized with mercury, weaned on lies. What once was rare is epidemic, now, among our clueless, introverted young. Must be the air, the water, something, anything. I dunno. Maybe it's the way we live. A language virus of the mind, like Burroughs said, you know? Yes. What else then? Yes, that's it, then. I'm certain. It's the way we live."

To the Bone

We entered Beauty to the bone and found the processes behind our dreams. The secrets machines share among their own. Input. Output. Error.

Truth is not beauty, nor is beauty necessarily true. Keats was a kid – alone, dreaming, mistaking technology (writing) for love and water.

"You're freaking out. What's wrong with you?" she said. "Something I did? Something I said?"

The arrogance, the vanity, the chutzpah of Love, passion, the lust to rut. Whatever. "What" is a name. Or can be. Once you've done your duty, served your pro-creative function, you can call your kid anything you want.

You're not who I thought I knew," she said.

I said, "I' yself alone."

"You're outer-space. Out there. I liked you better drunk."

The bone. The bone. The bone.

"Get out of here," she screamed. "Go be yourself, alone."

"Please. Let me…" I began. "Just let me use your phone."

My voice skipped 'cross the Nation, point to point, hub to hub, switch to switch, light speed.

"Hello," said a stranger on the other side. "Who is this? Hello? Hello? Answer me. Answer me."

"Are you crazy? Who are you calling? Where are you calling?"

"Answer me," demanded two strangers in unison.

Linked, connected, out of touch.

Underground

And yet another dumb protagonist, all inner life, asocial, dwells in tunnels built for trains the City has outgrown, forgotten. In darkest sanctuary, he dreams. Remembers. How long since the sky? Tunnels above him and The City above the tunnels and the sky above the City. Space. Stars and darkness beyond the Sun he hasn't seen in months. Maledictions of his species and the parasitic others that remain. Rats aloof, big as bears and vicious.

She comes to him with food procured by runners who deal daily with the light and traffic, hands and markets, of Above. He and She will never scavenge among them in the light, among them, in the noise. No, not again.

Better to Live, He and She, than to Survive.

The Long, Unhappy Globalization of Variable x

It began as a textbook case of mistaken identity: x for X, on a seemingly ordinary day, when parts of the world were seemingly at peace, oblivious to cars and children restless in back seats; rhetorical insinuations of policemen; Law Makers' official doggerel; the physician's scribble; how words escape into other words – not words, really: mute abstractions, tools of technique, signs of the literate beast: variables holding n to the nth power times their weight in imaginary increase.

Let x = turn_me_on_dead_man

Channel "x" through miles of circuitry pulsing with phrase: meaningless to untutored eyes; speech without sound, stripped integers, mute phonemes, cut vibes, signifying nothing, yet x obeys – because he's faithful, obedient, determined?

Worse: pre-determined: a shy, lost variable in a larger program than he could ever have imagined himself following, much less completing. Double-triple top secret MILITARY application, several million lines of code. Impossible for a local variable such as himself (trapped between brackets in an illegal function stolen from proprietary commercial code written, allegedly, to divert pornographic email ads from peeling virgin eye-lids) to know or even hope to understand.

Due to sloppy programming or, as is more likely, a malicious, intentional "bug," local variable, x, has been mistaken for global variable, X, possessed of privileged access, calls and pointers to every string, expression, numeral, every bit and byte of data in the OS, from command-line to kernel, up to and including floating points, slashes, blank white space, able to leap not only from line to line but program to program, even language to language without tripping test wires, alerting debuggers or other cautionary devices and details.

In other words, x, known now to The System as X, cannot be stopped, which is precisely why he must be stopped before the program compiles because… well, just because. That's how things work in this mad-cap world of military corporate techno-hocus-pocus, where even the source code is outsourced to slave labor or the cheapest, most downtrodden next-best-thing (patriots, heroes, persecuted minority groups newly "liberated") and no one sees the forest for the trees; hence, x, a minor, local variable, who signed on, originally, as a bit role byte in "Buck Rogers and Tar Baby: The Voyage Home," the final installment demo mock-up for a 3D gaming series, can be mistaken for X, an invaluable, invulnerable array of approximately 666 scaly scalars in the guidance system of the Ultimate Weapon of Mass Destruction.

Alas, poor x, I knew him …

Vroom, vroom Beautiful!

"Hard to recall the mortal me, watching movies on TV."

"Yeah, yeah," she replied. "Stay away from diet drinks and synthetic foods."

The old man lit a fire under the Victrola, summoning precious memories, smoke. Reached that age where even dreams and recollections are antiques. "Worth anything?" he wonders, thinking of old stamps and baseball cards. Surely there are at least a few dream-collectors with money?

Time passes frictionless, lubricated by our frivolity, numbness.

"I wanted to tell of my betrayal, but you being dead for years, it all seemed so pointless."

"…the fiction of the fiction that such a thing as dialogue existed once," she said.

He said, "I've dreamed the same celebrity dream everyone else has must be contagious."

She said, "I'm on stage and singing. Everyone loves me and they scream."

He said, "I'm on a talk show sharing my desires, angers, ambitions…"

She said, "Yes. Same dream. Makes me wonder how unique –"

He said, "It's the programming they program it into the television shows, commercials, magazines… billboards, radio, internet. No escape, really, unless you live in a hole, I mean if you…no matter where, you'll be exposed…"

She said, "Oh, nobody cares any more about the makers of dead things! The people who worked all their lives to get –"

He said, "Forget it, it's just a rage now all that rage…it's raw…the courage to perform laser surgery and say cool stuff like, 'Honey, I forgot to duck…'"

She said, "Do you really need to chew so much gum?"

He said, "Humor me."

Together they slept in the pink deeply, where everyone they'd known decayed, disappeared, no explanation…fade to black."

She woke up suddenly and said, "Decades burn like paper."

He rubbed his eyes and said, "When were you last called upon to do something important?

She said, "It used to feel so good to walk drunk in the dark city, before sundown…"

He said, "I'm afraid to be afraid. It seems like everything you fear eventually comes true. Once, it felt so good to breathe."

She sang a song dear to them both. He soon joined in:

Promise me we'll always love

Promise me we'll never die

Promise me you'll get off dope

Promise me beautiful

Promise me future

Promise me it won't all fall apart

After the singing, she panicked. "There might be focus, something to hold, I mean beyond machines in a cluttered office the laptops and cells when anyway you're remembering the day you danced on grave-markers those flat plaques, not to be mean, but because you felt so good to be alive and young and happy and occasionally you looked down and read how 'so-and-so was born and died and went on dates her favorite flower was a rose…'"

"Everybody has some good times tucked away," he said. "But now, the haunting: word phantoms; synaesthetic spooks of what was said and died approach in color."

Suddenly energized, she said, "Naked in the spot-light sun-light. The young are out today, displaying skin."

Somberly, he said, "The devastating scorch of passing. '…so you can't believe you're forty-five' the bank ad said. Only a little while, and then I'll be okay…"

Undaunted, she said, "Without fear of death, the cheer leaders suit up. Without fear of death, the smell of cut grass, leather…"

Smiling, he said, "The glare of car chrome on the highway, racing to good life…"

Together they sang:

"Vroom vroom, setting sun,

"Vroom vroom, beautiful!"

Westerners Dream Araby

What dream I had – or film? – of Westerners in Araby: 30s scene set in sepia streets of clutter-crash and rot. Hot. Hot.

Animals lope burdened, or seasoned, roast. Veiled women cook, singing.

Shirtless children sell anything-everything-whatever, screaming.

Fez Men, Fez Men, grinning.

Can't smell, can't; can't smell. Makes sense, non-scents flicker beyond linear Time of cinema/dream. Opium yen to (must I really really must I must, I must) inhale:

Anxiety burns. Misery. Streaks electric, magnetic, draw him to the light, where he will sizzle, in his colonial white suit.

Write After Eternal

Dear XOX,

Looking forward to your next adventure. Write me when you're about to begin again. Again. This time, hopefully, with Cosmic Eternal, not that slow decay that's – more or less – impossible to know other than data sputtered from ticklish instruments – absurdly expensive; glamorous; high tech. Thin margins of error noted with noble numerals of high birth and breeding.

Clock-tick, omnipresent side-kick, Time Observer lurks subjective: one with all you do. Tell me you've changed. That this is not another inquiry partial to "the facts," framed as they are, "forever time facts…"

Time is *not* forever, *not* objective, nothing but the figment of yet another, amateur philosophe probably, some third-rate Duke of X or Baron von Y, with leisure time to think, or pretend to, circa 1750. No dreams or experience, but thirteen prime rib stakes in Time Objective and Forever myth-seed of his puerile deity, the "way out there eternal, invisible, unsigned."

No, no-way, no, not this time, no. Nothing less than raw life, wild, born of genuine bad seed. No time for laws and other fictions. No tyrannies or Baronys of benighted square pegs.

Not again. No. No space for anything but real – congenital, organic.

And don't forget to write, once you're at liberty, completely unsettled and exposed.

Yours,

ASE

Ball-peen Oratory

> "Many think it not only inevitable but entirely proper that liberty give way to security in times of national crisis..." But, Scalia added, 'that view has no place in the interpretation and application of a Constitution designed precisely to confront war and, in a manner that accords with democratic principles, to accommodate it." —Antonin Scalia
> (http://www.newfrontier.com/asheville/terrorists.htm)

Sing, Muse, the anger of my hammer, smashing lineaments of star-crossed chancre-spotted love! Defacing faces; ball-peen tenderizing every kiss-me-cute television countenance ("somebody's baby, once") – chop chop – to goo of Human be. Mother of bad hair days; pulpy, resonant awareness of disfigurement, disharmony, disgrace.

Limp like laundry. Strewn in torsion, as if: spontaneous liposuction on the kitchen floor.

Rorschach for the house-bound failure; the asthmatic; the agoraphobic; the tired, huddled, massive masses, yearning to breathe free.

"You lick the blood off that floor. Now! Go on, lick it, lick it, do what I say, say, what I say and don't you dare do until I say."

Tastes like old hammer; tastes like blood.

Cursed with morning sickness, mourning sad. Breakfast candy myth of chewy-chocolaty divine rage of "who" not "what" rolled loosely within flammable, hammer-able, firm, yet vulnerable skin.

Somebody's baby, once, once someone's begin.

Killing Time

In Bright Engine Future gleamed the bright future of engines. Sunglasses invented to accommodate eyes still young and sensitive to the light of Truth (after all, it's only weeks since we left Plato's Cave), synthetic colors devised like prostheses reinforce lack of essentials. For instance the ability to interpret or even imagine the brilliance of our own design. We are a species, still alive, diminished, but not gone.

How long since I passed hedgerows scented with desire, basking in the simple, ample luxury of evening? Simplicity. Desire. Night.

And what is the color of fear? The Eyes' aversion to the mirror?

Oh for a cloth of fire to wipe away this misery, spread like contagion from overseas, from outer space, from Sesame Street, from Mr. Rogers' quaint, bourgeois den...

Most of our misery, the story goes, is home-grown and difficult to face without squatting behind a wall of terminologies, or slithering into the new vernacular, feigning bemusement and indifference.

"I've spent myself. Come. Go. Come or go, one or the other. Hectic, hectic, our so-called "'modern life.'"

Time purchased a train ticket, gave two weeks' notice.Killed a teenager at (where else?) Dead Man's Curve. Blood splattered Porsche. The girl walked away. Crimson head trauma. She could not recall the eyes or hair of her boyfriend, the desired young man, the dead one.COLD STOMACH, HEART OF CLAY, TOXIC BLOOD, read the headlines, referring to Time's condition at the scene. News reports alleged Time left behind an indifferent wife.

Why dwell on tragedy? Sunny, cool, perfect weather for a football game, for it was Saturday. But the first-string quarterback had died, the night before, in his father's Porsche.Golly.

But good news. Very good news indeed: the second stringer made the day, threw three long touchdown passes and scrambled for a third (plus two-point conversion) to mention but a few of many extraordinary feats. Twenty completed passes for more than 300 yards and not a single interception – rare for high school play. They won with big numbers, carried him on padded shoulders, doused him with celebratory Gatorade.

Time, unsung hero of the day, sped on. One-way ticket to The Future. No return.

Here

Here: where parents outlive children, fathers weep over puddles that once walked as sons.

Words stick like glue in the throat, despite recorded sightings of ether-phrases "in-between," you know, like physicists see particles where most see nothing but what's "really there."

The laughing ones who drank us under tables: under ground now, cold as stone, nibbled by creatures nourishing their young (yet more moist life, tubular, disgusting).

The dead are gone, yet debates continue, unsettled, round by round. For instance: the girl on the beach, no longer slim, young, pretty on the sand, compelled Yesterday to Dream lubricious rumbas, roses crushed in tango teeth, around the pretty young girl on the sand.

Better yet:

The man in a fedora chased the woman, whose derringer held secret data: why do men crave females in pheromone sombreros? They stopped, embraced, tip-toed through Georgia, eloped under UFO-light to star-struck Tennessee. These "occurrences" are what we see and feel and touch – not physicists plucking quanta from dark metals, or sentences silent in deep tissue buoyed to ear-level by poets, who hear them slither through gray-matter like worms.

"Here" is a chain of painful links, that will endure until the final syllable is swallowed by the fattest, wettest life, and all finality is finished. Really.

C'est toot.

The Science of Forbidding Fruit

We are forever opening doors and falling from windows into situations we are unprepared to claim; nevertheless, we steel ourselves, bulwarked by culture, and certainty that facts comprise systems greater than their sums, that these systems are themselves the sum of knowledge.

The science is irrefutable: a man on the moon is worth ten in the bush.

There can be no compromise, no hesitation of belief. Credibility demands credulity: science is power; might makes right; what we know can never hurt us (so long as what we know is all we know and ever will).

Our meaty diets must be clean of hidden fiber and forbidden fruit. This vinegar Despair, distilled of sadness, bad wine of knowing, bruised fruit of occurrence, a product of Now's bitterness, can be traced, like most others, to sweet-blossom origins of empty.

There was a time – many times, in fact, all done now, finished – it could have gone one way, or another. This was "this," or possibly, just possibly, it was "that."

All depends on outlook, and can change, since it is not knowing, really, to simply know what's "known."

Focus on in-look, not out-look. Outside is Always, and will always change, but Inside is finite and shapes its own narrow Outside according to plasticity of True within.

Not outside looking in; snatched glimpses of random distortion; no real significance; but inside looking out, projecting your immutable True upon the ever-mutable There.

You know?

For instance, that crap about the "dead king" sacrifice. Jesus's appeasing his mean Old Man for the sins of mankind in order to save mankind was not as wickedly conceived as the mind of mankind is capable of and consistent in conceiving.

Men hate and fear god. The way they hate and fear The Corporation. And like The Corporation, God is invisible, immortal, untouchable. But Jesus, his tender, proxy on earth, was quite mortal, visible, touchable. Better yet, he was capable of being harmed, of feeling the spectacular intensity of human pain.

So men nailed him to a cross, their only redress against the merciless, implacable, unreachable God-The-Father. Dad.

Our Own

Lead us beyond frightened gardeners, boot-steps deep to real; Judges; land "Lords;" "those who would be taken," suckered, ushered. Love's squalor and ideal betrayed with arbitrary fruit, pink-slip codicils to freedom (as possibility): as if: my kingdom," my kingdom for" a hearse, or Paradise for obscene visions, barren buildings, sealed deposit boxes centuries to come: echo of sandal-slap footsteps down long-shadow corridors and no vocabulary to describe the idiocy, the paper.

For instance:

They can count you on their fingers, but won't bother, though this is the digital epoch of fingers, spiders, creepy crawlers. Watch them crawl the creepy creep across the kitchen floor. Ten ten ten ten ten over and over. Your head is meaningless. They won't hear you; they won't see you; they're autistic, and they're in control. It's maddening, I know but it's the way of things. And they're our own.

My what big guns you have. Is that battalion REALLY yours?

They won't answer. They won't bother. All the money in the world, to them, is merely all the money in the world. Enough to drive a thinking feeling breathing one insane, but see what good that does. They'll walk right through you as they look right through you without knowing feeling smelling hearing sensing you in any way.

They won't hear you; they won't see you; they're autistic, and they're in control. It's maddening, I know, but it's the way of things. And they're our own.

They don't know who they are themselves, why bother counting you?

After all, a finger is a finger and a rock a human tree. Animals and paper planes light up the sky with rocket blood storm cataracts. Why not bark at skyscrapers and genuflect to Baal? The toenail you won at the Fair and flushed days later cause he ate too much you fed him bread.

Alligators in the sewer ate the New York Mets. The artichoke-banana-fig band plays this Cosey Island of the mine.

They won't see you; they won't hear you; they're autistic, and they're in control. It's maddening, I know, but it's the way of things. And they're our own.

You can't leave. "Away" is gone forever. Blood bombardment is the only game in town. They own the team, residual rights to recollection. Every game you've ever seen (I hope you saved your ticket stubs;come tax time you'll need proof). You're thinking, "I can reason," hoping to appease. It's like that "Twilight Zone" when Li'l Opie wrecked the planet with his evil childish bad seed mind. Wished to "the corn field" any adult whose stomach disagreed with peanut butter hamburgers and ice-cream.

What's in the cornfield? You ask though you don't really want to know. They can't see you; they won't hear you; they're autistic, and they're in control. It's maddening I know, but it's the way of things, and they're our own.

You don't want to think about anything because they know when you're not thinking their thoughts. They know — and they don't like it. If you're not thinking their thoughts, whose thoughts are you thinking? More importantly, "why?"

If you're not thinking their thoughts, maybe you *hate* them; maybe you want them *gone*; maybe you don't want them back again *ever never ever*.

This upsets them. Though they won't see or hear or count you, they want you to love them always or be dead. Love them like you've never loved anyone, ever, or be dead.

They won't see you; they won't hear you; they're autistic, and they're in control. It's maddening, I know, but it's our only ALL. The only thing of which we can be absolutely certain is the absolute power of "our own."

Ready, Able, Fire

God Bless

(this christian nation brought to you by desert nomads from outer space, who augured our future in seventeen organic lentils that clung to Essau's beard – you can look it up: read your Koran, your Talmud, your No One Here Get Out Alive: Pilgrims in UFOs; Cowboys in Stutz Bearcats: sorry red injun man, sorry black negro man, sorry yellow asian man, sorry women and children first in line, fists full of soap, tossed overboard: the Ship of State can't help you now. Apparent misreading of the roadmap begotten yet another snafu epic nowhere, but *they* are everywhere: you've seen *them*, I've seen *them*, everyone always sees *them*. Why won't *they* leave? Until they're gone you'll have to grin and bear it, elbow grease your hair, tuck "Lucky's" up your shirt sleeves, genuflect before the one and only undisputed heavy-weight Lady-Liberty-Turned-Golem, marching off to smite *them* and every last one of *them* among *them*. Save us all—in proper hierarchies of ascent—from biased prosecution. Smile and be clean. Say yer prayers, the pledge, anything that pops into Brave Leader's mind and sticks— like pigeons in peanut butter; like maggots in honey; like dinosaurs in tar—and for gods-sake remember: cameras roll all the time now, cameras roll all the time now, cameras roll all the time now, and they just might roll on over you, so wear your Colors and be Mighty.)

us, everyone—*them* too, after they're dead—amen.

Unfamiliar as a Stranger's Dream

What is this this Nation, unfamiliar as a stranger's dream? Don't be mortal, don't, don't. Find someone nude to touch. Flesh-candy. Firm as children.

The CFO poured over quarterly profit margins. Laughed himself to sleep at his desk. Awoke screaming. Cried for himself and lost profit. Cried convincingly for others.

This Nation of bah-sheep shorn again. Fleeced multitudes flee white magic. Notorious wanting. Insipid pretense of "I need." Daily routine. Money comes to them, harnessing extremes, inciting laughter.

Directed away from, not toward. Heroes don't pay rent. Bills accumulate. Read the papers. See us famous. Yesterday, yesterday, but what have you done for us lately? Cheap block paragraphs talk black and white. Newspapers don't lie, news-makers do. Simple constructions blown out of proportion.

Guns don't kill forest fires, news-makers do. Anywhere everywhere always, even here, especially here, at a theater near you. Become a millionaire. Meet zealous partners, enemies, lovers, friends.

Smells even worse at the gym. Personal trainer, full membership. Show up 12 times join forever, or 12 times quit, it's your call. Slide your card to prove attendance or no money back. Cash from your card at the forever and a day machine. Satisfaction guaranteed. If you lose the weight, you must be satisfied, so no money back. Believe me, once you're in, you're in. On every continent. No easy contract.

Join the gym, be fit for life. Fit like handcuffs. Does this strait-jacket fit? Receive a tooth or fang with *your* name on it. Custom-cross commemorating your personal crucifixion. An autographed magic bullet. Hollow point DU. Splash effect – inside and out. Cameras pan eyes not dead yet. Glossy-glassy like a donut, glazed. Now *that's* dead.

Your name on it. Member of the seven mortal gyms. Crowded too, and sweaty

Phantom the Hotel

Sweat-hot breathed her skirt. A starlet's countenance and stamina to flirt the night away, gassed on lust, youth, grit. Drank free — exchange rate: tongue or glimpse of tit. She stunned salacious passersby and shadowy voyeurs with her narcotic spice of core perfume. No games or cocktail talk: she hungered. Feel first, taste, then smother. Birds in nougat bowers chirp drunkenly what's past, what's passing and to come. Chocolate towers slouch toward gingerbread Byzantium. Mock on, mock on: another season's entertainment. Here and Now is All, she knows; she burns both ends, but slow, man, slow.

Beneath Us

Forget littered with and/or comprised of strings, runes, tablets, funny faces, symbols, letters, hieroglyphs pretending to know sound and sensibility in real time, myth and meaning in mute construction. Numbers, really, when dismantled to the nit-grit, dis-covered and dis-clothed down to the base mint.

This is the digital age (true there are digits under the hood: one zero on off blip blink mumble "Melancholy Baby," baby, and I'll toss you a figure-head coin) but what we see and hear is what we know and will recall. We're on our way to real, in 3D no less, on every flat screen large and small, however many bits and bytes rage in mute assembly under the hood.

Program

Protagonist, star of our book, was blond, muscular but not grotesque, six feet tall, the perfect hero. Don't you think? Body of rich earth, feet of clay. He worked at the recycling plant, smashing bottles against a wall. He listened to music while he worked. One day, as if out of the blue, (though it had been simmering beneath consciousness like garlic in cheap oil) everything in his fragmented life, in particular the sum of its parts, the jagged jigsaw whole, seemed pointless.

"Do you enjoy your job?" the Company Shrink asked.

"Hell yeah," said Protagonist. "I think. Maybe. Really, I don't know."

After his breakdown Protagonist read novels. In bed. Words marched in dense but orderly narrative formation across thin leaves of paperbacks. No one came to set them free. Protagonist, who had never experienced plot or narrative in his own life, was utterly miffed by The Nature of the Problem. Variables involved. Parameters. Otherwise, what good is a solution that can only be understood by a few specialists living in other dimensions?

He turned his attention to computer Programming, which better matched the circumstances of his condition. The programs themselves, that is. As written by Programmers. The end result, events unfolding on terminals and screens, in text or GUI, meant absolutely nothing. He studied both Functional and Object-oriented Programming, envisioning himself as an object whose ultimate purpose was to function.

At the Cemetery of Peace and Silence, Protagonist accidentally slipped into another life. Rose Vestinger, 1940-1995. A clearish, warmish old-fashioned day at the beach when Rose was thirty and tending her husband and two small sons. Idle talk in short loops, easily escaped. Sun tan lotion. Salty breeze. No soap, radio. A day in this stranger's life, circa 1970, revealed nothing to Protagonist, still recovering from his breakdown.

No soap, radio.

Bored, he turned to the computer itself, the machine. World Wide Net. Myriad connections. Sticky Spiders. Big mistake. Flashing whirligigs, mob-ocracy, Programs turned to products, commodities, and animated by other scripts owned – it never says "invented" – by the same few corporations. And much like the television he despised, the damn thing would not shut up.

Alone in a room with rambling screens and no ideas. Waiting. For what? For some kind soul with the ability to act? To pick up the remote and shut the damn things off forever? All of it? Control-Alt-Delete? Kill -9? Shutdown? Or whatever command for *death* (of the mere process, or the entire system?) the lingo of your Operating System happens to obey?

Dark Above Her

Twenty-five years ago the beach. Sun rise. Pumped. Coppertone. Valium. Don't panic. Really, they're only life-times. Before the photograph you couldn't recognize years passing, one after another. The records. Watch us watch ourselves grow old, starched white sheets and all.

Without logic or intensity, we sought mountain stature, draped ourselves as if the world could end this way, in the boudoir, where dogs bark fantasies and women weep for virgin days of Summer, water-melon, songs around campfires (real or imagined), marshmallows burnt to ash but soft inside, white, sticky.

"They were huge, enormous, and they multiplied," Madame said.

After the party, cocktails. Pure in the beginning, we spit on their ashes, escaped to yet another…"this is the guest-room."

Anticipate agony. We know no other way.

Generic Memory of no particulars. No individuals or details. Just what The Race knows and remembers.

"Same thing, same as your…"

"Calm down," she said. "Relax. It was all just skin."

But her 100-pound tumor sprouted hair and teeth. Every moment's ugly creeping till the floor drops. Beneath us we see red.

"Have you been working out?"

"She really does look thin."

It's instinctual, the rage. I want to kill him whenever we're close. Enough soap operas and narratives. Paint me colors. Sing me songs. The way things turn. I never wanted to be like this. One of those fuck-ups who can't tame Life.

Day is torture, unbearable. Night skips, like a record.

He was a matador of speech, assuming, as we did, conversation to be the seminal art form.

Eventually we all know peace. Or at the very least ignorance of, or indifference to unrest.

And all the years passed through the fiery-minute of a dream. Algorithms of Time known only in sleep.

Staggering, the countless lifetimes spent in bed.

"And dark was above her in the sky."

She reached the very end, the intensity of faith, absence of fear and other intimations of freedom that surface to awareness when there's absolutely, positively no place left to go.

A Very Brady Homeland (the lost episodes, circa 1968-73)

Arise Jan, Marcia, Cindy! Arise Greg, Peter, Bobby! Arise Mike, Carol, Alice!

Vbh.X.118: In Country

The soldier in the bush does not forgive. All is not well with us, not always – what do we know from love? To reach informed decisions among fraudulent sources; that momentary rapprochement with the species – after all it is our planet, in some ways, but we are only the people, our leaders, responsible adults, architects of our…

…the photograph of my mother in a drawer somewhere I never saw again…I know there is a center and I'm walking toward it: union of man and woman for perpetuation of…genocidal tendencies. If only it were simple as fallen cake. Blonde girls, dark boys; the servants ignorant and happy. Tiger lies among the lambs while we devour similar illusions. In love with youth and freaked out by corruption. The judges scratch out every line. "Be fruitful and multiply (but don't be fruits)," and all this happens over Sitting Bull's corpse (or some slain Injun under the cement). What we were thinking, that is, we must have known… in the beginning…

Vbh.X.119: Bobby and Cindy Emerge

And love abounds, again, to conquer all together now we're Sgt. Pepper's Lonely Hearts Club Band, again, the letter, the word, can tear us apart: missive misconstrued, one must read between the lines, the meaning of the text must be resolved, that is, our children must be protected from the… doors of perception bolted shut. All we wanted was a bond, a union. Nobody cares about us but us, though occasionally a Stranger rides to town, rids us of doubt. We search our pockets for a tip. Pennies later, Silver gallops down the street. Neighbors complain. Manure on the pavement gleaned by complainers for their gardens; minutes dry like raisins under ersatz sun. Divide them evenly among ourselves, chew twenty times in unison, swallow, like a family, for real, this time…

Vbh.X.120: Mike and Carol Remember

The children were playing when you mowed the lawn. Cut-grass memories of milk; recipes for drinks with mint; cakes colored like moods. Youth isn't forever, it is now is the time to make things. Can you concoct gourmet cuisine while designing your bedroom to appease Pat Nixon? If so, don't bother me. I value comfort over pretence, lifestyle over life for style. Fruit salad, garden-grown arugula, a tart or cobbler made from plums. Adam and Eve bounced from Eden and that spiteful land(lord) screaming, "Die!" and "Get ye jobs!"

We return to the garden, also to labor, but our work is pleasure. We find enjoyment in our skills. We don't believe in peanut butter, per se, but we believe in peanut butter cookies. We believe in the inherent worth of stuff around the house. We believe in using stuff to construct other stuff. Food is not for thought, food is thought. We adapt to the fickle appetites of children. We don't demand roses without thorns, but we prefer them, and though this is "The Information Age," not all information is of our age. Sometimes it's good to work with wood. Sometimes "going digital" means working with your hands to build an edifice worth overtones of Maxfield Parish, incest...

Vbh.X.121: Greg and Marcia lost in the Black Forest, Malibu, Muscle Beach

A clean backyard bereft of possessions. Left to our own, we lived on magic. Pain beyond description. Plummeting gut-feeling of "to have, but-not-enough." Trail of bread-crumbs, sweets, that bird we saw, an instant. Mother said, "No, no..."

We wanted to behave. So difficult now, after these years, to recapture rage. No matter what happened, forces beyond our control: addiction, attachment, recipes for disaster. Only sacrifice, pulp from the heart, will make us new again, that kind of soft, sentimental tolerance. Day-to-day awareness of your you. Again, it's hard to go back, even in trance. Blood rivalries, fantasies of dominance, submission...but there were reference points, a general context. Actions mattered, or so we believed. A family, an institution. Hierarchy – we at the bottom, out of control. Our only option was to live...

Vbh.X.122: Peter looks out the window.

After the killing, respite: small talk, smokes, lock and load. We sought to eliminate the root of our misfortunes. The cop held the law like an umbrella. Belief in magic powders. Mother came back from the dead to fetch her cigarettes. Everything ablaze – the ranch house, the backyard. Children threw textbooks at the fire. Why can't we be healthy? That is, released from our addictions:

masturbatory visions of his sister's naked "what about your homework?" but we'd already studied that dull certainty what more could they want of us? fighter planes flew overhead on secret missions overseas respect the might of the Nation be thankful our problems have been (thus far) trivial bright future, tons of it,

so long as we stay very, very young...

Vbh.X.123: Cindy's Big Audition

The performance yielded no salvation. Not even God could attend. When we were young, we sang without afflatus. Money came. Mary Pickford curls. Eloquence matters. Your big eyes and cutie-pie smile – who could resist? All that fades. We thought children mattered, that is, it mattered to be clean. There could be no conflict, no ashes to ashes, no dig your own ditch, kneel, await bullet smash warm balloon skull...

Vbh.X.124: Greg and Peter leave the house, but return in time for dinner.

Gut-feeling of doom. Seemingly, all is well: refrigerator stocked with the usual fare; nevertheless, we're hungry. The newspaper arrives on time each morning. Cheerleaders bare tasty thighs, encourage us, onward alma mater smash that opposition, fodder for slaughter. The scoreboard counts the ways. Our (compound) fractured goals– snapped femur jagged splinter rip through skin and cotton. Preparation: sit-ups, push-ups, sprints. Summer, before we were strong. Accept the ball and run with it. Wanted to lie down and sleep, right there, on the grass but home is no place for quitters. Water and oranges; whistles, grunts, cheers. Our mothers brought us lemonade and tea. The soft life. Promises. Our first great leap toward pussy...

Vbh.X.125: Marcia! Marcia! Marcia! and Greg dreams...

Not everyone is innocent. Nightmares of goose-stepping marauders. A single pubic hair curled out from her bikini. She isn't of our blood, merely our brood. Rebel within us but to cringe like that, to bow...Papa, papa – strike me! Kill the father, take the girls, erect a statue. Not easy to deal with, these cascades of desire. Concentrate on work. The day will come when we will leave this place, our faculties intact. Such a small garden for youth to unfold, yet, we are told, we will have memories. We look to the future but one day we will look back at the past and doctor it according to our needs. So we are told. I believe in neither the future, nor the past, only the tits next door, burgeoning, blossoming. Flower metaphors old-fashioned, but pertinent. Throwing tennis balls at the garage door, practicing my curve, not overly conscious of the self. Now I am awkward at dinner, spilling milk. Silverware in sweaty palms. Small talk, furtive glances. Some kind of...I don't know...society...civilization, and we its discontents. Father, pops, 'dear old dad,' says "Where would we be without our laws?"...

Vbh.X.126: Alice Out of Uniform, At Ease

Not quality of life, surveillance. Epic flight. Spray fear on the fire. Lemme tell you 'bout "the day." Electric scent of ions. Panic in the air, or creativity. Anyway, night comes. Spark the tube. Crack a brew. Relax.

Vbh.X.127: Greg and Marcia meet again

Superb thugs, elegant masters of brain judo. Has it been so many years? We grew tired, traveling far plugged in, connected. I remember when…a dime to hear your voice…not the same since you earned your degree. People yearn for healthy snacks, cults beckon. Your thesis on thought control and mass society. The media drone on and on. Still, we learn some things. I wasn't afraid of the dark, I just preferred the light. Energy diverted. All that garbage in the meadow. "Burn it," she cried. We chose oxygen. She said, "You'll rue the day"…

Conquering armies raided our kitchen. Afternoons of plenty. Paisley, flowers, suede. We watched our denim fade. Almost soul-mates, sharing the toilet and the maid. Ruthless hazing of neophytes. Your beauty saved us from remorse.

Vbh.X.128: Boys and girls in separate rooms

Napalm next door. Another channel. The family room. Potato chips, popcorn. Hand in her lap. Cathode mirror screen float leisurely on heated gene pool. Variant DNA – it's kosher. Pump, squirt, moan. Logistics. Cards, cake, talk… talk…won't endure. But to be certain. But to think. Our right to watch ourselves on television. All decisions, the important ones, blown. Absent a Cosmic CEO, we've run amok…

Vbh.X.129: Greg and Peter on the beach; Jan and Marcia wade into the vast Pacific

Grim but certain. Ghastly. We are inured. Weather reports predict a house of pain. The test returned positive: life produces life. But when we…the doctor implied there could be problems. What were they thinking, we think, as we scan the old photographs. We can never really know what it was like to live in that time, though we ourselves lived in that time. The artifice of memory cannot be learned. One must be born prone to illusion, a type of genius shared by all, at one level or other, but wait – I've seen that face before. That punim stirred the lava of my apprehension. But I was young then, like the face, which is young no longer in the world of mutability beyond film. Such instances of – what would you call it, delight? – make us wish we were dead…

Vbh.X.130: Family Trip

Like clowns in a small car, we formed special bonds, honked for direction; stopped, interrogated, produced ID. All papers in order. My brothers, my sisters.

Mama, papa. Stale bread and cheese. The trout are dead. We whistle in the dark, afraid of beasts in this protected wilderness, courtesy Ted Roosevelt, big game hunter, like Hemingway, but made of stiffer stuff. Olfactory rush. Nose like a raccoon. I smelled her hair. Pulsating glands. The price of gasoline. A memo from the President: search and destroy…

Vbh.X.131:   Jan, Peter, Bobby, Cindy, on a picnic, laugh about the past

Scream as we may for ice-cream, we demand novelty, choice, butter-fat not withstanding. Cereal box promises. Send your name, address, favorite singer and, of course, proof of purchase. Reward you with amusing – never much good: snap-together tchotchkes smashed in a day, neutralized. Impatient for the mailman nonetheless. We fought over flub-dubs. Plastic, sugar-dusted. Authority malfeasant from the top. Trickle-down cascade of corruption. Buy our nutrients. Cherry crème formula to tantalize your tots. Just say "no" to dugs…

Vbh.X.132 :   Carol's "hot flashes" and mood swings

I don't pretend to know how women's bodies work, I merely own one. Next time we'll go cruisin.' I haven't met a single…I don't respect many…there comes a time…I've been meaning to…yes. Out in the world, the children, the broken whatcha-ma-call-it, hold me. I'm determined. I hate my lawyer, daughters, vows. Never sent me anything I wanted. Look at me. Listen. When it was possible to choose, I never – the station-wagon, the counter-top, linoleum, Windex, suitcases; ginger-beer and rum dark as molasses. Ordinary…plain…the sun shines only on stars. Dreaming of cigarettes a decade smoke-free. That boy who set the movie-house ablaze yelled "Fire!" in a crowded theater, and he meant it, and saved many lives. Growing old in the nut-house, the asylum. His mother… stomach trouble, she claimed. Our narratives, our situations, subject to debate. The telephone won't stop. Cheerleaders…firemen…the virgin werewolf scratching at my door…

Vbh.X.133:   Mike drinks absinthe at the bowling alley

Too many, six billion, to reconcile with government, democracy, tax shelters, food and the rest. Pledge allegiance to a cloth. Hide our hearts with our hands and warble. Wave yet oe'r the land of brave red rockets. Relax girl, when it's your turn, when it comes, you'll be dead forever. I too was lost, for a while. One mind reading silence of eternal inward. Dreaming of you. The question of morality. All that controversy about – chastised by the network. "Unhealthy relationships," they said.

The bartender said, "Los Angeles." She sipped her very pink cocktail. "Constantly," the bartender said. "She can't stay away…from trouble…"

Vbh.X.134: The family breaks; the children go their separate ways

I dreamed America put on weight. Huge calico frock. Massive flesh bucket of lethargy and tears. Liberty in her cups. Denatured nectar. The man on the train went on and on about markets, portfolios, preferred stock…

Another day the waterfall.

You *thing*—"qualify, propose, negotiate, close"—you *thing*—of…you…

Abraham & Franz

How long since Kafka served Lincoln in the New World, at Civil War, when Kafka led murderous troops from Georgia to Paris? Stonewall Jackson died and Lee released the dove. Abe and Franz shared a succulent blood orange of victory while Grant swayed drunkenly at "attention."

Though many historians pay hard attention to the manic, melancholy life of Lincoln, they neglect to mention his blazing orange bowtie and his boon companion, Kafka. nor have any written of Abe's love for Dove Ice-cream bars consumed outdoors in Paris.

Kafka's dream was to win in love, like Paris, whom he much preferred to Menelaus. "Attention: better to woo Beauty, soaring graceful like a dove, than win her through grim slaughter, eh, Lincoln?" said the hopelessly romantic General Kafka. Lincoln, depressed, beat Custer with an orange.

When a special White House screening of A Clockwork Orange failed to break Abe's mood, they tried Last Tango in Paris. Abe remained sullen, and all eyes turned to Kafka, who chose a pen and paper as his locus of attention. Finally, a smile stretched the brilliant, goofy face of Lincoln. When razor-toothed Ozzy bit deep into a dove, and scrubbed the black blood away with moisturizing Dove. "I'd like to show that fellow my heavy metal orange T-shirt, but he's a big celebrity and I'm just Lincoln," said Abe. "One day we'll share café-au-lait in Paris. But so many loose ends, like Civil War, merit my attention. If only I could delegate the heavy stuff to Kafka.

That idea for a Penal Colony for recidivist Rebels was pure Kafka. Yet Kafka was too busy reading Pynchon, Kleist, Wings of the Dove, and orchestrating trials and executions at the Castle, to pay attention to weary Lincoln's yearning for simplicity and Duck L'Orange. But finally Franz assented to an all-expense paid trip to Paris and the two packed beer and snacks into Honest Abe's used Lincoln.

The trip was dreary for Kafka. He threw Cheez Doodles at Lincoln, who lost his attention at the wheel and crashed into an orange crate, liberating a dove, which morphed into a Beetle over Paris.

Let Me Bequeath

Box me on a warm bright day, hands folded over thousand dollar shirt and tie. Let me hear young things on the grass plan parties, raves, getaways with only legal, ethical narcotics. Or Booze.

Dress me well! Indulge me in their rites of coquetry and intrigue, nasty gossip, sing-song music and doomed dreams.

Grant me peace in my silver suit. Close the plain pine lid and lower me down by crane.

Let them be curious, perhaps, almost, fearful...

Gather them here to wonder: why consider "future," after all? Let it all be so alien to them, the sky so clear.

Leave them to savor aromas of skin and spring; befuddle them with magic, music, pheromones and beer; celebration of lips and hair; lusty minds a-flirt with promises –

I'm done with all that. I wish them well.

Corpus: Language of the Future

Silent is the language of command. The program. Java, C, Python. Dialects of the machine. The Masters scour data bases with regular expressions honed to pin-point accuracy. ASCII octal numerals in unicode convey multiple meanings, but no sound. Symbols but no sound. Unless we imagine haunted screams of special characters and typed variables muffled by the disk drive hum –; hummmm–; hummmmmmmmmmmmmmm–; illusion of free association snared in skeins of code: open the trope, unravel the rope: links to poison applets: you are what you eat, if you can catch it.

I have studied the code, and imagined rhythm, meter, lines read aloud, modulated, enlivened, like poetry, by the human voice. As if pure mathematics could be sung or chanted, evoking all of the latent power and simplicity of the abstract, numinous meanderings brought to earth as mass and sculpted to the simplest, most elegant equations.

$E=Mc2$ F minor. How many fractals in a Violin Concerto? Do we get extra points if we win? And so on. The root of "program" comes from the Late Latin word, "programmus," that is, "to state or proclaim in a speech or address," something along those lines.

CODA

I have bad habits
but the trees
are aware of their green today
and the check is in the mail
and the sun is drunk and loutish
in the marble
sky.

www.ingramcontent.com/pod-product-compliance
Lightning Source LLC
Chambersburg PA
CBHW071718040426
42446CB00011B/2113